The author on board H.M.S. *Velox*

Routledge Revivals

The Latvian Republic

First published in 1965, *The Latvian Republic* is based on the official British documents, partly on German and other writings of the period and of the author's own experiences on a mission to Baltic Provinces in 1919. Throughout the centuries of foreign domination and the determination of their rulers to stamp out all vestiges of nationalism, the national spirit of the Latvian people survived, and they remained united in the hope of achieving, one day, the state of independent nationhood. With the collapse of the Russian Empire towards the end of the First World War, their dream became reality. A Latvian Provisional Government was formed and in November 1918 the Latvians declared themselves an independent republic, encouraged by the declaration of President Wilson in favour of the self-determination of all peoples and of all nations. This book will be of interest to students of history and political science.

The Latvian Republic
The Struggle for Freedom

Herbert A. Grant Watson

First published in 1965
By George Allen & Unwin Ltd

This edition first published in 2024 by Routledge
4 Park Square, Milton Park, Abingdon, Oxon, OX14 4RN
and by Routledge
605 Third Avenue, New York, NY 10017

Routledge is an imprint of the Taylor & Francis Group, an informa business

© George Allen & Unwin 1965

All rights reserved. No part of this book may be reprinted or reproduced or utilised in any form or by any electronic, mechanical, or other means, now known or hereafter invented, including photocopying and recording, or in any information storage or retrieval system, without permission in writing from the publishers.

Publisher's Note
The publisher has gone to great lengths to ensure the quality of this reprint but points out that some imperfections in the original copies may be apparent.

Disclaimer
The publisher has made every effort to trace copyright holders and welcomes correspondence from those they have been unable to contact.

A Library of Congress record exists under LCCN: 66003396

ISBN: 978-1-032-74356-1 (hbk)
ISBN: 978-1-003-46890-5 (ebk)
ISBN: 978-1-032-74359-2 (pbk)

Book DOI 10.4324/9781003468905

THE LATVIAN REPUBLIC
The Struggle for Freedom

BY

HERBERT A. GRANT WATSON
formerly of His Majesty's Diplomatic Service

DEDICATION BY
THE LATVIAN MINISTER IN LONDON

London
GEORGE ALLEN & UNWIN LTD
RUSKIN HOUSE MUSEUM STREET

FIRST PUBLISHED IN 1965

This book is copyright under the Berne Convention. Apart from any fair dealing for the purpose of private study, research, criticism or review, as permitted under the Copyright Act, 1956, no portion may be reproduced by any process without written permission. Inquiries should be made to the publishers

© *George Allen & Unwin Ltd*, 1965

PRINTED IN GREAT BRITAIN
in 11 *point Old Style*
BY UNWIN BROTHERS LTD
WOKING AND LONDON

DEDICATION BY THE
LATVIAN MINISTER IN LONDON

It gives me great pleasure to commend this book of the vivid personal reminiscences of Mr Herbert A. Grant Watson, concerning his Mission to the Baltic States.

As a former British diplomat, it was Mr Grant Watson's fate to play a unique part in the events that attended the 20th century renaissance of the ancient Latvian nation, who proclaimed their independence on November 18, 1918.

Now that the Baltic States have again come under the forceful occupation of a greater power, there are some 120,000 Latvians scattered in exile all over the world. A number of them are still in urgent need of the charity of their fellow men. I am most grateful to Mr Grant Watson that he takes a generous interest in the peoples whom he first knew in the days of their hope and achievement, which will surely come again.

CHARLES ZARINE
Latvian Minister in London
January, 1960

NOTE

The question of the names of places presents a difficulty. The former Germanic names are familiar to English readers and are still widely used in English publications. They have however been replaced by Latvian names, which of course appear on the Latvian maps. In my narrative I have used the Latvian names, except in the historical chapter, but I have given in brackets the old Germanic names. The chief changes are the following,

Old	New
Courland	Kurzeme
Livonia	Vidzeme
Frauenberg	Saldus
Goldingen	Kuldiga
Kovno	Kaunas
Libau	Liepaja
Memel	Klaipeda
Mitau	Jelgava
Reval	Tallinn
Windau	Ventspils
River Dwina	r. Daugava
River Windau	r. Venta

I have used the term 'Balts' to denote the landowners of Saxon or German origin, frequently known as the 'Baltic Barons'.

I have used the term Latvia in preference to Lettland and Latvians in preference to Letts, although both are correct and are given in the Oxford Dictionary. The modern form, now in general use, is Latvia.

I have used the form Estonia rather than Esthonia, although again both forms are correct.

CONTENTS

Introduction	15
1. *The Baltic States declare their Independence*	17
2. *Latvian History*	26
3. *German Policy towards Latvia during First World War*	35
4. *Fighting in Kurzeme (Courland) between Germans and Bolsheviks*	39
5. *My Mission in Lithuania*	47
6. *German Coup d'État in Liepaja (Libau)*	53
7. *Germans flout the Armistice of November 1918*	58
8. *Policy of White Russians towards Baltic States*	64
9. *Battle of Cesis*	65
10. *Germans prepare to move East*	71
11. *Battle before Riga*	78
12. *Independence of Baltic States*	86
13. *Baltic States absorbed in the Soviet Union*	90
APPENDIX	95
BIBLIOGRAPHY	97
CHRONOLOGICAL TABLE	99
INDEX	101

ILLUSTRATIONS

The author on board   *frontispiece*
  H.M.S. *Velox*

View of Riga   *facing page* 56

M. Ulmanis and the Latvian Government
  land at Liepaja (Libau)   57

MAP

The Baltic States   *pages* 24–25

INTRODUCTION

In 1919 as a result of the great upheaval caused by the First World War, three new nations rose to the international surface and their names were inscribed on the new map of Europe. They were the so-called Baltic nations, Estonia, Latvia and Lithuania, and I was sent by Lord Curzon, who was Foreign Secretary, to visit these countries at the time of their formation when they were coming to life. Each country had a separate nationality, preserved intact through several centuries, during which they had been ruled by powerful neighbours who had kept them submerged, without power of expression, mere provinces of great empires. However, they became independent nations, and for twenty years, 1919—1939, flourished as separate states, with all the attributes of sovereignty. They despatched diplomatic missions, they concluded treaties, they attended international conferences, and then on the eve of the Second World War they again disappeared from the map of Europe. Their disappearance was not due to any internal weakness, political or economic, but rather to their geographical position. They were placed within a zone which Russia came to regard as her military zone of defence and as the Russian rulers decided to take complete control of that zone, these three independent nations were again absorbed in the Soviet Union.

Lately I have had the opportunity of studying the carefully collected papers published in Volume III of *Documents on British Foreign Policy* 1919 edited by Sir E. L. Woodward, M.A., Professor of Modern History in the University of Oxford and Mr Rohan Butler, M.A.,

Fellow of All Souls College, Oxford. This volume covers the period when the three Baltic nations were struggling for their independence and brings to the knowledge of the student of history the official documents dealing with events in the Baltic, including despatches etc., preserved, in the archives of the Supreme Council in Paris, official correspondence from the archives of our Foreign Office and War Office and correspondence from our diplomatic and military missions at various posts in the Baltic. Many of these papers, some regarded as confidential until now, have remained hidden in archive rooms and libraries but have now been released and made known through the labours of the editors to all those interested in the events of that period.

As already stated, Volume III deals with the complex situation when the Latvian Republic started on its career as an independent Republic and this short book has been built up partly on the documents published in Volume III, partly on my personal experiences when I was on mission in the Baltic and partly on my knowledge of events as they have developed in that area.

Some of the material given in this book was included in a small book published under the title *Mission to the Baltic*.

The German War Office in Berlin published in 1937 and 1938 two volumes regarding the fighting in the Baltic States in 1919, from the German military point of view. These volumes can be found in the British Museum but, so far as I know, have not been translated into English.

CHAPTER I

THE BALTIC STATES CLAIM INDEPENDENCE

My Mission to Latvia

While I was serving as Second Secretary at our Legation at Copenhagen towards the end of the First World War, a long succession of delegates from the outlying nations of the Russian Empire came to Denmark and visited the Allied legations in order to put before them their plans for establishing independent national governments and to request recognition by the Allies. Foremost of these were the Polish and Finnish delegates, but others included the Ruthenians or White Russians, the Estonians, the Latvians (Letts) and the Lithuanians. At that time the Russian army was in full retreat and the centralized bureaucracy of the Russian Empire was disintegrating, and those nationalities which had never been assimilated to the great Slav state and had looked forward to the time when they could become independent and manage their own affairs, realised that the long awaited opportunity was approaching and that they must prepare to assert their rights as separate nations. By now they were confident of the victory of the Allies and knew that to them would fall the task of resettling the boundaries of the European countries. In November 1918 Germany at last acknowledged defeat and sued for an armistice. The Allies then set to work to draw up a new map for Europe.

After the conclusion of the Armistice one of our first acts was to send two squadrons of cruisers into the Baltic

THE LATVIAN REPUBLIC

Sea, to re-establish our sea power, to open up those waters to our shipping and to establish contact with the new nations which were coming to life along its shores.

The first Allied naval force to enter the Baltic was commanded by Admiral Sir A. Sinclair, and Admiral Sir Walter Cowan followed a little later at the head of his squadron, the First Cruiser Squadron. He had recently brought his ships into the harbour of Copenhagen where a number of entertainments were given in his honour. We had occasion to meet frequently at lunches, cocktail parties, etc., and one evening when I was with him on board his flagship, H.M.S. *Caledon*, he suggested that I should accompany him as his guest during his forthcoming voyage when he intended to call at the port of Liepaja (Libau) where the Latvians were organizing a provisional government. My chief, Sir Charles Marling, gave me leave of absence, and so, early in February 1919, I sent my luggage to H.M.S. *Caledon* which was moored at the Lange Linie, and the Commander, Captain Wallace, kindly placed a cabin at my disposal. Naval officers, who are kindly people with a natural wish to help their guests, are excellent hosts. I had my meals with the Admiral in his private cabin, but I spent much time in the wardroom where the officers congregate when off duty. They lent me a revolver from the ship's stores, but fortunately I never had occasion to use it, also a marvellous mackintosh lined with sheepskin, which I found invaluable during my travels.

Since 1916 the Germans had been able by the extensive use of mine-fields to close the Baltic to the ships of the Allies and, when the Armistice was signed in 1918, the mines were still in position, unswept and untouched. Our Admiralty obtained a chart showing the passages between the mine-fields and this enabled our ships to penetrate into the Baltic. Our relations with the Germans were governed at that time by the terms of the Armistice, but

BALTIC STATES DECLARE INDEPENDENCE 19

with the other great Baltic power, the Bolsheviks, we were in a state of war on account of their challenge issued to all rulers when they called upon the workers of the world to unite and overthrow their rulers and governments. However, except on one occasion when two or three Bolshevik destroyers approached the Reval Roads and attacked British destroyers, the ships of the Bolshevik navy remained in harbour and avoided contact with the ships of the Allies.

On leaving Danish waters the flagship proceeded with extreme caution, the bows protected by paravanes and the gun crews at their stations. We followed closely a red line on the chart, indicating a narrow passage between the danger-zones. It was dangerous to deviate in the slightest degree from the course and the ships which did so almost invariably ran into mines. The Captains tried, if possible, to sail only by daylight and to reach port before dark, as it was easier for them to take their bearings in the daylight. In July Admiral Barry Domville allowed my wife to make a short trip on H.M.S. *Curacao,* but when that cruiser sailed on another voyage and under another commander, the latter left the red line so as to cut off a corner and gain time to reach port before dusk; the ship struck a mine and was lost.

Admiral Cowan gave me the run of the ship and invited me to the bridge where, just before dark, I saw a curious phenomenon. Straight in front of us a thin white line was discernible on the water and I heard a voice mutter 'the beach'. I felt certain that we were heading either for a sand bank or for the low-lying coast of northern Germany. The Admiral and the Captain peered ahead through their glasses but did not betray any sign of emotion; a few minutes later our bows broke into the white ribbon, which turned out to be a fringe of small pieces of ice, evidently broken off from the edge of an ice floe and which by some trick of the current or the wind had remained in this unusual shape. Several officers confessed to me that they had their hearts in their mouths but they concealed their feelings most effectively. We were still at sea during all that night and early the next morning entered the roadstead before the port of Liepaja and anchored. The narrow channel leading to the inner harbour was covered with ice but the hardy local pilot, a Dane, broke through with his ice-breaking tug and came out to us. I went ashore in his boat, accompanied by Mr. Vivian Bosanquet, who had been our Consul at Riga and who was also sailing on H.M.S. *Caledon*.

In spite of great difficulties, political and economic, the Estonians, Latvians and Lithuanians had set to work to build up national governments, free from the control of either Germans or Russians. As early as July 1917 the Estonians had formed a national council, charged with the duty of creating an independent republic, but a few months later their country was occupied by German armed forces and, by the Treaty of Brest-Litovsk of March 1918, the Baltic States, including Estonia, were ceded to Germany. When Germany collapsed a few months later, Bolshevik armed bands returned to Estonia and overran the country. A number of refugees were able to cross the Gulf of Finland to Helsinki, where they were well received and, when the Estonians appealed for military help, the appeal was answered with enthusiasm and two Finnish volunteer regiments and a few batteries were organized with the utmost speed. The Finnish units landed in Tallinn (Reval) on December 30, 1918 and were immediately engaged in the counter offensive planned by General Laidoner, commander of the Estonian troops. The campaign continued with increasing success throughout the whole of January and the greater part of February, until on February 24, 1919 General Laidoner was able to announce that the country had been freed of the invader. Estonia had declared her independence on February 24, 1918.

BALTIC STATES DECLARE INDEPENDENCE 21

On November 18, 1918, a few days after the signature of the Armistice, the Latvians had formally declared their independence. Riga, and later Liepaja, were the seats of their provisional government. Their country, Latvia, consisted of three provinces, Livonia, Latgale and Kurseme (Courland), but when we arrived Livonia and Latgale were occupied by the armed forces of the Bolsheviks, whose roving bands had penetrated also into Kurzeme, as far as Jelgava (Mitau) and Ventspils (Windau), while the rest of Kurzeme, not occupied by the Bolsheviks, was under the military control of General von der Goltz, Commander of the German army of occupation. His headquarters were also at Liepaja.

He knew of the arrival of the Cruiser Squadron and of the fact that Bosanquet and I had come ashore, but we could not foretell whether he would allow us to enter the city. According to the terms of the Armistice, all German troops, beyond the German frontiers, were to return to Germany when the Allies so demanded, but General von der Goltz had openly defied the orders of the Allies and of his Government and was in the position of a rebel. Nevertheless he expected that the Allies would overlook his disobedience. He regarded the Bolsheviks as a threat not only to German but also to European civilization and was convinced that the Allies would hold similar views. As he commanded the best trained and the best equipped army in eastern Europe, he anticipated that they would even make overtures to him and commission him to drive back the Slav hordes who were endangering the whole of Europe. Probably for this reason he allowed Bosanquet and myself to proceed to the city and meet the Latvian ministers, although he knew that our visit would give great encouragement to the popular campaign for Latvian independence and lessen his authority and perhaps interfere with the movements of his troops, who were engaged in fighting the armed bands of the Bolsheviks.

However, when we left the quay, the German sentries saluted and we entered the city on foot, making our way to the offices of the provisional government. M. K. Ulmanis received us and explained in detail their plans, and we also met prominent people who were outside of politics. In the evening we returned on board H.M.S. *Caledon*, but next day we landed again and continued our conversations with the Latvians. We handed in a short report to the Admiral, which he relayed by wireless to London, and the squadron left the harbour and returned to Copenhagen. A few days later Sir Walter received instructions to take his ships again to the Baltic as it was feared that the Bolshevik fleet would leave their Russian ports to make a demonstration in the Baltic and even in the North Sea. He took his squadron to Hangö, a port on the coast of Finland, and settled down to blockade the Bolshevik ships shut up in the harbour of Kronstadt.

I resumed my duties at the legation and a few weeks later received instructions to proceed to Latvia and Lithuania, to establish informal relations with the new governments and Mr Bosanquet received instructions to proceed to Tallinn (Reval) to watch the situation in Estonia. The Peace Conference had assembled in Paris and were demanding reports on the happenings in eastern Europe, so unofficial agents were sent out to gather information. I embarked on H.M.S. *Galatea* and returned to Liepaja. Admiral Cowan stationed a destroyer, the H.M.S. *Velox*, in the harbour to act as a guard ship and, as the military and political situation was so uncertain, the Captain, Captain Burges Watson, gave me the use of his sea cabin, to keep my papers and my correspondence.

On account of its fine natural harbour, Liepaja had developed both as a commercial port and also as a naval base which the Russian Baltic Fleet used in winter. Along the sea front, with its fine stretches of hard sand and low sandhills and dunes, well-to-do Russian families had built

BALTIC STATES DECLARE INDEPENDENCE 23

solid wooden bungalows and summer residences which, in spite of their primitive appearance, had comfortable living rooms and were well heated even in winter. The residential quarter was laid out with small parks and gardens and, further inland, a few factories had been built, with rather ill-kept primitive workmen's dwellings. Beyond was fertile country. A British Intelligence officer, Major Keenan, had arrived before me and, as the Latvian Government had placed at his disposal one of the larger summer residences, he invited me to share his villa. He had been in the flax trade before the war and had made several firm friendships with prominent Latvians who kept him well informed of the situation. He was thus in an exceptional position to estimate the various currents and counter currents at work. At that time, food in the markets and in the local shops was scarce and difficult to purchase, so we lived chiefly on army rations kindly supplied by the Navy.

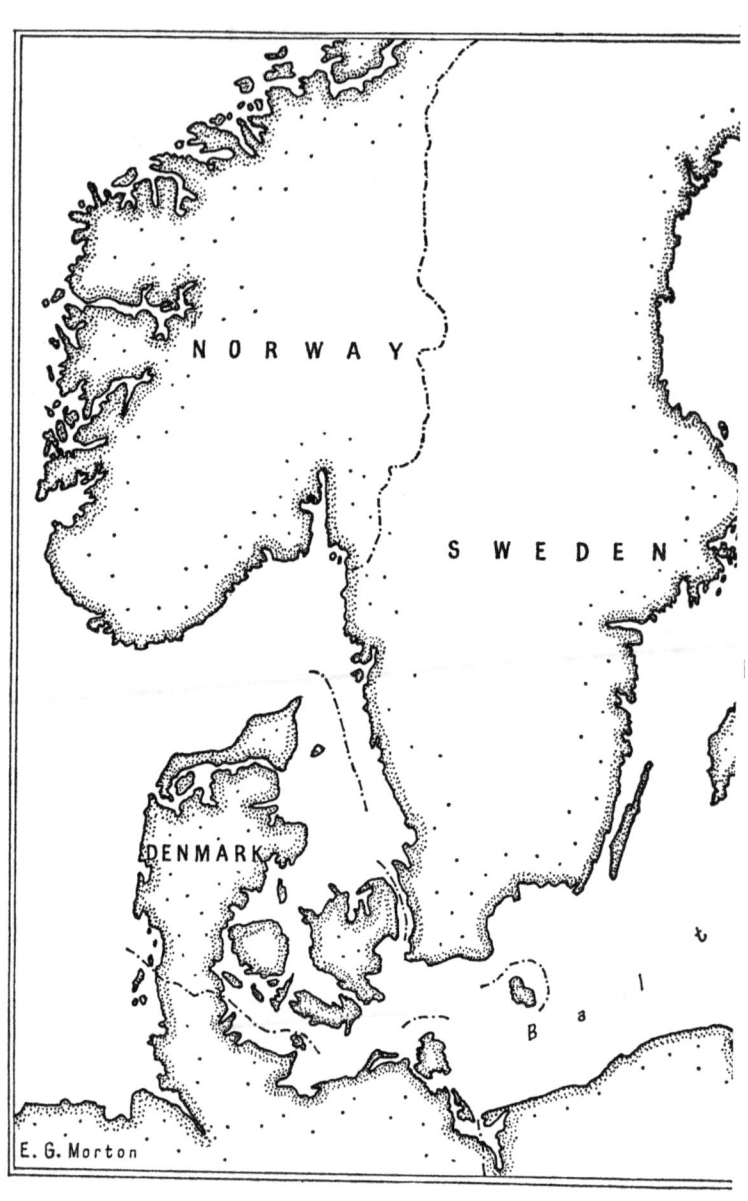

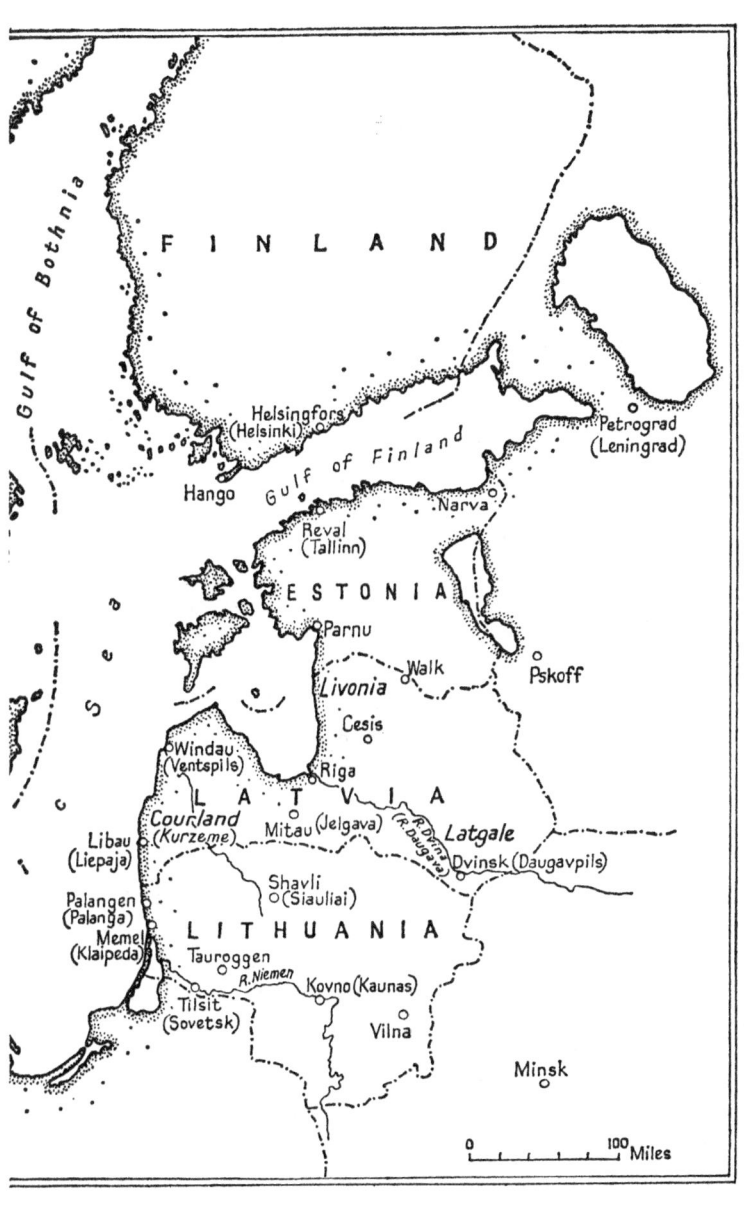

CHAPTER II

LATVIAN HISTORY

In order to understand the peculiar position of the Latvians in 1919, it is necessary to look back on their history, which is also of a peculiar nature. The Latvians and the Lithuanians belong to the Indo-European group of nations, distinct from both the Slavonic and Germanic races. Very few of the inhabitants are of Slavonic origin. The Latvians are closely associated with the Estonians but the latter belong to the Finnish Ugric family of nations and have a different origin. The population of Latvia was about 2 million, of whom 76 per cent were Latvians, 10 per cent Russians and 3 per cent Germans. They belonged mainly to the Lutheran Church and only 4 per cent to the Russian Orthodox Church.

I mention these figures to show that the Latvian people, in spite of long periods of Russian and German domination, in spite of wars fought out in their territories, and in spite of serfdom and even slavery, remained a closely knit and compact nationality.

The Latvians had been settled for a long period in the region of the Upper Dnieper and in the eighth century, under pressure of other East European tribes, had been forced to migrate in a north-westerly direction until they reached the southern shore of the Baltic, in the neighbourhood of the mouth of the river Daugava (Dwina), where they abandoned their nomadic way of living and settled. They assimilated the inhabitants of the coast, the Livs, who were of Finnish origin. The Latvian tribes were well-organized politically, but had not been welded into one

LATVIAN HISTORY

nation before the Germans obtained a footing in Livonia and later in Kurzeme (Courland). With the German pioneers came priests, who sought to convert the Latvians to Christianity, and also merchants from Bremen, Lubeck and Wisby in Gothland, forerunners of the great traders of the Hanseatic League who established trading centres along the coast. In 1199 the pagan chieftains in Livonia rose in arms against the Christians, who refused to pay tribute to them. In consequence the Pope decreed a Holy War against the pagans in the Baltic. Doubtless he was moved by the desire to prevent the spread of the Byzantine Church's influence in these territories and to win them over to Rome. In AD 1200 Bishop Albert of Bremen sailed up the Daugava with 23 ships and a large concourse of German adventurers, under Count Konrad of Dortmund. The knights who took up arms on behalf of the Christians received from the Pope all the rights and privileges of crusaders and were enrolled in an order, called the Order of the Military Knights of Christ. This was suppressed in 1236 and the knights were incorporated in the famous 'Order of Teutonic Knights' one of the great military religious orders of the Middle Ages. The Teutonic Knights were under the special protection of the German Emperor and were exclusively of German birth. Riga was founded by Bishop Albert in the following year. The new city's statute was copied from that of Wisby in Gothland and German masons and artisans were invited to take part in the building.

The great period of expansion of the Order was in the middle of the thirteenth century when, under the leadership of Henry of Hohenlohe, it established itself on the Baltic coast to fight and convert the pagan Prussians, Latvians and Estonians. The Order however never penetrated further East beyond the frontiers of the Baltic Provinces and it never entered Lithuania, which lies between Prussia and Latvia. In 1254 both the Pope and the Emperor confirmed to the Order its possession of lands in Kurzeme (Courland) and Latgalen. The Latvians resisted for 100 years. Their tribal or clan organization, however, was a source of weakness and in 1290 they were finally conquered. Local Latvian councils and institutions were abolished and all distinctive forms of national life were suppressed. Livonia and Estonia were united in a federation, ruled by the German bishops and nobles, under the supreme direction of the Grand Master of the Order who resided at Marienburg in Prussia. For many years Livonia served as a barrier against the Russians and other Slav invaders and halted their expansion towards the West. The knights provided the heavy cavalry and the infantry was composed mainly of mercenaries.

The Teutonic Order had been founded to conquer and convert the pagans and when the Baltic peoples entered the Roman Catholic Church, its original purpose ceased and it assumed the duties of protector of eastern Europe. In reality the knights became feudal landlords, with the rights and privileges of feudal 'seigneurs'. By its constitution however the Order was incapable of founding a national administration and the knights never bridged the gulf between themselves and the native people. They always remained foreigners in the land and this was the cause of their final downfall.

The merchants of Riga developed the old trade route along the valley of the Dwina and established direct trading relations with Russia. In 1280 the city entered the 'Hansa League' and as a large volume of Hansa trade from east to west and from west to east passed through this port, their prosperity greatly increased.

Papal legates, on instruction from the Pope, informed Bishop Albert and the Brothers of the Order that converts should not be deprived of their personal freedom and property, and in 1232 the Emperor Friedrich II ordered that the new converts should remain free subjects of the Holy Roman Empire. These orders however were disregarded by the knights, who reduced the Latvians and Estonians to a state of serfdom, so that their lot was miserable in the extreme. Their status varied according to the period and according to the district but for the most part they were attached to the soil (period AD 1494) and they had to work as many as five days a week for the seigneur (1500). The general attitude of the Order towards the Church was one of complete disregard.

When German influence declined, the Swedes crossed over the Baltic and established themselves in Estonia and at the peace settlement of Vilna in 1582 which terminated the Livonian War, Livonia was divided between the Swedes and the Poles. Kurzeme (Courland) became a semi-independent duchy under Polish suzerainty.

The period of Swedish rule is called by the Latvian historian, Professor Schwabe, the 'Happy Epoch', as the Swedish rulers helped the local inhabitants and encouraged their cultural development and education. The peasants were still attached to the soil but they were assured of their land and their position was greatly improved. The private justice of the nobles was restricted and the dreaded *jus vitae et necis* of the landlord over the serf was abolished. Efforts were made to raise the status of the Latvian peasants to that of the Swedish peasants, but they were not successful as the resistance of the Baltic nobles was too strong.

A few days before the Battle of Lützen in 1632 Gustavus Adolphus signed the deed for the founding of the University at Dorpat, for the study of Protestant theology. Teaching was given in the Estonian and Latvian languages and the sons of peasants were admitted to become pastors. Communal schools were opened in each parish and three secondary schools at Riga, Tartu and Tallin (Reval), to which the sons of peasants had access. In 1687 the Bible was translated into Latvian at the expense of the Swedish King, Charles XI.

As a result of these measures, the Latvians became more conscious of their racial origin and nationality and the separate tribes and clans joined together and became welded into one nation. However the powerful foreign nobles still dominated the administration and the Latvians were only allowed to play a very minor part in the affairs of the provinces.

After the battle of Poltava in 1709, at which the famous Swedish army was destroyed, the generals of Peter the Great entered, conquered and devastated Estonia and Livonia, which were ceded to Russia by the Treaty of Niestadt. Owing to the fighting and the pestilence and famine, the people of these provinces were in a lamentable condition and the famous message sent by Field Marshal Scheremetieff to the Czar—'There is nothing left to destroy in the country, except Riga and Tallin'—(Reval) shows the miserable straits to which the inhabitants of this fertile country had sunk.

Although the nobility was reduced to 172 families, only the nobles had the right to sit in the Landtags and they became the real masters of Livonia. They treated the Latvian peasants with great brutality and practically made slaves of them; the landlords could buy and sell them, just as if they were part of the equipment of the farm. 'The Estonians and the Letts are slaves, not persons; merchandise, goods which one sells or exchanges', wrote the German Pastor A. Hupel in 1777 and Professor Schwabe quotes the Italian traveller Le Clerc (*Storia della Russia* 1785) as writing 'In Livonia and Estonia the nobility is everything. It is the Government and the State. The duty of the people is to feed the seigneurs, who can sell them and separate them from their wives and their families. They are afraid of everything, except death.'

In all their dealings with their serfs, the nobles were

LATVIAN HISTORY

above the law and as late as 1762, Catherine II declared that there was no law by which a noble who was guilty of killing a peasant could be condemned.

The Duchy of Courland flourished as a semi-independent state from 1561–1795 and was ruled first by the Kettler dynasty and later the Biron dynasty. It was spared many of the tribulations of Livonia and developed as a prosperous agricultural country. A large element of the population was attracted to a sea-faring way of life and Courland developed and manned an important mercantile marine. Windau became a busy centre for the construction of vessels, both ships of war and trading ships. Under the famous Duke Jacob, Kurzeme (Courland) acquired Gambia, a colony on the West Coast of Africa, and later the island of Tobago. These colonies were only held for a short time but they are striking evidence of the enterprize of the Courlanders in the eighteenth century.

At the time of the final partition of Poland in 1795, Courland, with the whole of Latvian territory, came under Russian rule, and thus three countries, Poland, Lithuania and Courland, disappeared from the map of Europe.

The Order of the Teutonic Knights was formally abolished by Napoleon in 1809, but the Baltic nobles remained in control of the provincial and local governments and later the Governors-General appointed by the Czar were usually Baltic Germans. The nobles kept possession of their estates and even regained some feudal privileges which they had lost. However, in the course of the nineteenth century, the lot of the peasants gradually improved. For the first time in history the Latvians were united under one government, albeit a foreign government, and this unity was a source of strength. In 1819 serfdom was abolished in the Baltic Provinces but the peasants were still unable to obtain land and their lot did not really improve until after the agrarian reforms of 1860, when a class of Latvian small landowners was created.

This was the beginning of the economic freedom and self-dependence of the Latvians.

The Russians allowed the Latvians to keep their distinctive customs, language, etc., until 1889, when they tried to assimilate the provinces entirely with Russia proper. Russian officials, Russian judiciary, and the Russian language were introduced and the new policy was aptly expressed by the motto 'One Czar, one Church and one language', but the Latvians resisted this pan-Slavic movement, just as they had resisted that of the Germans. They opposed the new Russian officials, just as they had opposed the German Land Marshals.

The Czarist Government made fitful efforts to curtail the privileges of the landowners, and in 1888 manorial justice and the rights of the police were transferred from the nobles to the Russian officials; again in 1893 committees were formed to represent the Latvian peasants, but the nobles continued to oppose these liberal measures and were successful in maintaining many of their old privileges. For instance they maintained the sole right of establishing breweries, distilleries and public houses on their estates, and in spite of great opposition kept this right until the Lettish struggle for independence.

The Lettish farmers were further helped by the spread of the co-operative movement and by the founding of Loan Banks and thus they obtained the means of purchasing more land and of becoming the owners of the farms which they worked. By the opening of the twentieth century, they had acquired about 40 per cent of the agricultural land, and as they became more prosperous so the standards of education in the schools rose and the Latvian educated class become more numerous, more influential and more active. They kept their own customs and spoke their own language and became increasingly conscious of their national unity. They felt they were sufficiently advanced both intellectually and economically to demand their autonomy or even to separate from Russia. The 'Latvian Workers Party' received strong support among the people and its aim was to free the country both from the Russians and the Germans and to claim independence. As they could not hope to obtain this, while Russia was ruled by the Czarist autocracy, their leaders supported the democratic movement in Russia, so also the Latvian movement for autonomy increased.

The defeat of Russia in the Russo-Japanese war in 1905, gave the Latvians the opportunity to rise in revolt and they fought under the red flag of the parties of the Left. They attacked all the Russian institutions and also those of the Baltic aristocracy, and in the country they burnt down the manor houses and destroyed the property of the nobles. The latter appealed to the Czar for protection and regiments of Cossacks and Dragoons were sent, who suppressed the revolt with much bloodshed and cruelty. The breach between the Latvians and the Baltic nobles was still further widened.

At the outbreak of the First World War, the aims of the Latvians and the nobles, still the dominant caste, were so widely divergent that they were practically in a state of civil war. The Latvians demanded the right to establish an independent or at any rate an autonomous state and their claims were supported by the more advanced parties in Russia.

The Czar refused to make any concession to the Latvian nationalists, except to authorise in July 1915 the enrolment of eight Latvian Rifle Brigades, under Latvian officers, with the commands given in the Latvian language. These brigades fought with distinction against the German invaders and later, after the collapse of the Czarist empire, their reserves were used for building up a national Latvian army, though some of the units remained in the 'Red' army.

The publication of President Wilson's 'Fourteen Points',

including the right of self-determination for all nations, greatly encouraged the Latvians in their campaign for independence and, after the Bolshevik 'November' Revolution in 1917, they decided to separate from Russia. They had no sympathy with the excesses of the Communists. A provisional Latvian National Council was founded at Walk with the object of forming an independent state. By this date the political parties were well organised and represented all sections of the people, both in the town and in the country. They united and formed a 'democratic bloc', to carry through this task. Riga was still occupied by the Germans, who did not oppose them openly as they hoped to win them over to their side, but the Latvians rejected decisively the Brest-Litovsk treaty by which Russia ceded the Baltic provinces to Germany and the relations between the Latvians and the occupying power became very tense.

CHAPTER III

GERMAN POLICY TOWARDS LATVIA DURING THE FIRST WORLD WAR

During the First World War, the German policy of expansion towards the East varied according to the success or otherwise of the German armies and the advance or retreat of the Russians.

The Diaries of Admiral von Muller, Chief of the Naval Cabinet of Kaiser Wilhelm throughout the First World War, throw an interesting sidelight on the plans of the Kaiser and the High Command for German conquest in the East, especially as regards the annexation of Latvia and Estonia.

In November 1916, before the collapse of the Russian Empire, the German Chancellor informed Baron Burian, the Austrian Foreign Minister, that the German government's eventual terms for peace would include the annexation of certain areas of Kurzeme (Courland) and Lithuania for the purpose of rounding off the German frontiers in the east.

However, in July 1917 after the first Russian Revolution, the Kaiser travelled to Jelgava (Mitau), the capital of Kurzeme (Courland), where he received a delegation of the local nobility and informed them 'I abide by what I have previously stated, i.e. that Courland would be German.' Later in August he again stated in regard to Kurzeme (Courland) 'Where my bayonets are on guard, the land will under no circumstances be returned to the enemy.'

In February 1918 the Soviet delegates met the Germans at Brest-Litovsk with a view to concluding peace between

Soviet Russia and Germany. Trotsky, the Soviet delegate, declared that hostilities with Germany were at an end, but he refused to sign a treaty of peace containing the German terms for the annexation of all the Baltic territory as far east as Lake Peipus and including Latvia and Estonia. In consequence of this refusal, Hindenberg and Ludendorff, the German High Command, called for immediate military action and an advance towards the north-east, with the occupation of the Baltic Provinces.

Hindenburg affirmed that the German minorities in Latvia and Estonia were threatened by the Red armies and that it was his duty to protect them. His proposal was opposed by Count von Hertling, the German Chancellor, and Herr von Kuhlmann, the Foreign Secretary, who feared that a German advance would precipitate the massacre of the German settlers. In the end a compromise was arrived at and a declaration was published repeating the German desire for an armistice but stating that German troops would advance as far east as Walk, that is to say that they would abandon their previous plan of an advance still further eastward to Lake Peipus. The military occupation of this former Russian territory was of a temporary nature only, made for the purpose of protecting the Germans who were threatened with violence.

On March 3, 1918 the Soviet delegates were obliged to yield and to sign the Treaty of Brest-Litovsk, by the terms of which Latvia and Estonia were ceded to the Germans. The treaty was ratified on the 17th.

At the close of his Diaries in October 1918 Admiral von Muller bitterly laments the fact that, after the collapse of Russia in 1917, German armies on the Eastern front were not released to fight on the western front but were employed in the conquest of Estonia and Latvia. This mistaken policy he attributes to the megalomania of the Kaiser.

In their policy of expansion towards the east the

GERMANY POLICY 37

Germans were aided by the Livonian Landtag, which in March 1918 proposed to the Kaiser Wilhelm a personal union with Kurzeme (Courland) and Vidzeme (Livonia), and invited him to accept the Ducal Crown, and again in December 1918 the Livonian Land Marshal, Herr von Stryck, conspired to bring the Baltic Provinces under German rule and offered to the Duke Adolf Friedrich of Mechlenburg the title of prince. The conspiracy was discovered when the papers of a Swedish Lieutenant-Colonel Edlund were seized as he disembarked in Libau. Von Stryk's letters to the Duke Adolf were published but it is not known whether the latter consented to the proposal or not.

It must be added that many of the Baltic nobles fought with distinction in the Russian army and rendered great services to Russia but on one policy all the nobles were agreed, and that was to prevent the formation, by hook or by crook, of independent Estonian or Latvian Governments.

When Germany collapsed and the victory of the Western Allies was assured, M. K. Ulmanis, the leader of the 'Peasants Union', formed a coalition of the Democratic parties and, with the support of the National Council, established in November 1918 a provisional Latvian Government in Riga. M. J. Tschakste was nominated as President and M. Ulmanis became Prime Minister, M. Z. A. Meierovics, Foreign Minister, and M. Walters, Minister of the Interior.

The German Government recognized the independence of Latvia and Estonia and appointed Herr A. Winnig as their diplomatic representative to the new Latvian and Estonian Governments.

Herr August Winnig, who was destined to play an important part in the events which followed, combined the Office of Ober Präsident of East Prussia with that of German representative to Latvia and Estonia and resided at Koenigsberg. At Mitau his Chargé d'Affaires was Herr Buchardt.

He had succeeded Herr von Batocki as Ober Präsident and for a short time had continued his policy. When East Prussia had been dominated by fear of the Polish army and also by fear of a Bolshevik invasion, Batocki had worked for the formation of a Statenbund or League of States, consisting of East Prussia, Lithuania, Kurzeme (Courland), and Estonia, free of both Germany and Russia, but the plan failed to receive support in East Prussia and Lithuania and was discarded. The chief power was to reside in the hands of the large landowners. Although he was a Socialist, Herr Winnig continued to support the great Balt landowners in Kurzeme (Courland), because of their German origin.

The German Government also supported the 'White' Russian organizations, who fought for the unity of the Russian Empire and were opposed therefore to the independence of the Baltic States.

In spite of these and other contradictions, Herr Winnig remained a dominating figure in the government of East Prussia.

CHAPTER IV

FIGHTING BETWEEN
GERMANS AND BOLSHEVIKS

Great Britain was the first of the western Allies to take a practical interest in the struggle for freedom of the three Baltic peoples and to realise that they had advanced sufficiently to form independent nations, capable of deciding their own political future. For centuries past it had been natural for the British people, on account of their own struggles for liberty, to view with sympathy and understanding the struggles of small nations to obtain political liberty and justice. In the nineteenth century they were on the side of the South American colonies when they broke away from Spain and gave their wholehearted support to Canning who 'called a new world into existence', so also they approved of the policy of Lord Curzon who helped the border states to throw off the yoke of Russia. In 1919 the epic civil war in Russia was being fought to its grim conclusion and we knew that, at that time, neither the 'Whites' nor the 'Reds' were ready to recognize the independence of any of the border states. The 'All Russian Council', of which Monsieur Sasanov was Chairman, was tied by its formula 'the indivisibility of Russia', and refused to make the slightest concession to this principle, while the policy of the Bolsheviks was to overrun all three Baltic countries and win them over to Communism. In order to help the Baltic countries to drive out the Bolsheviks and the Germans who again invaded their territory, we despatched military and political missions to them, and we supplied them with arms, ammunition and military equipment. However we did nothing to interfere with their relations with 'White Russia' and abstained from granting absolute recognition of their independence. Nevertheless, my appointment was regarded by them, as it was intended to be, as a *de facto* or provisional recognition and as such gave them much satisfaction.

During my interview with the Latvian ministers, they explained to me that their immediate aims were to obtain recognition by the Allies, to be freed from the blockade which we maintained in the Baltic and to receive a loan or credit to enable them to purchase foodstuffs and military supplies in Scandinavia.

Shortly after my arrival in February 1919 I forwarded to the Foreign Office the application of the Latvians for the removal of the blockade, and this was granted. Latvia had been practically ruined by the 1914-18 war and many fertile districts, especially in Kurzeme (Courland), had been devastated by the armies. A number of peasants had left their farms, which remained abandoned, and in the towns also the population had greatly diminished. For instance the population of Riga, which before the war had stood at 516,000, was reduced in 1919 to 225,000. Consequently foodstuffs of all kinds were lacking. In Lithuania, however, in spite of hostilities and in spite of a lack of workers, the harvest was the best within living memory, and a surplus of grain was available for export to Latvia. American relief supplies soon arrived in the Baltic and their value amounted to nearly £7 million. Supplies in smaller quantities also arrived from the United Kingdom and from Sweden. The transport of these supplies was carried out largely in British ships.

The United Kingdom granted credit to the three Baltic states for relief purposes but by 1920 all three countries as regards food were self-supporting.

The American Child Feeding Organization fed and

FIGHTING IN KURZEME 41

clothed 80,000 children in Estonia, 80,000 in Latvia and 20,000 in Lithuania. The Latvians also applied to us for arms and ammunition to enable them to carry on their fighting with the Germans and Bolsheviks and we supplied a considerable number of rifles. Further shipments of arms however were subjected to long and unexplained delays, as even at that date Communist agents were busy in our ports, endeavouring by all possible means, including sabotage, to hold up all exports of arms which could be used against the Bolshevik forces.

As I have already mentioned, Bolshevik ragged armies had advanced in a south-westerly direction across Livonia and had reached the River Daugava (Dwina). In February 1919 they occupied Riga, where their famous Commissar, P. Stutzka, a Latvian lawyer, took over the administration and ruled as dictator. The Russian armed bands then crossed the Daugava and advanced westwards as far as the River Venta (Windau); among the towns which they occupied were Ventspils (Windau), Kuldiga (Goldingen) and Saldus (Frauenberg) and at the beginning of March they were within 50 miles of Liepaja. Elated by the easy success of the revolution in Russia, the Bolshevik leaders had planned to stir up and provoke revolutions in other countries and to encourage peasants and workers in eastern and central Europe to rise up in rebellion, overthrow their rulers and Governments, and seize power for themselves, as they had done in Russia. Their army was ill-disciplined and ill-equipped but their faith in their creed and their self-confidence were unbounded. They believed that they had only to appear in the Baltic countries and eastern Germany and that instantly they would be acclaimed as liberators by the toiling masses. The Latvians, however, determined to oppose their further advance. The sturdy peasants intended to defend their land and their individual rights and those of their nation. They rejected the Communist doctrines and were prepared to organize an army to fight the Bolshevik army. Colonel Kalpaks was the founder of the Latvian army and he organized the so-called Kalpaks battalions. Unfortunately he died on March 5, 1919. A more important obstacle to the Bolshevik advance was the army of General von der Goltz whose advance guard held Jelgava, only twenty miles distant from Riga. General Count Rudiger von der Goltz was undoubtedly a great political general, far-seeing and firm of purpose. In the First World War he served his government well. Before the Armistice he had landed in the South of Finland to assist the White Finns under Field-Marshall Mannerheim to clear the Bolsheviks out of Finland. The Germans arrived too late in the field to play a large part in the fighting, but Germany gained credit by the expedition. On February 1, General von der Goltz was placed in command of the German troops, numbering about 25,000 in Latvia and Lithuania, but while the German armies in the west accepted the Armistice, he refused to acknowledge defeat. At the head of a group of arrogant officers who had never been defeated in battle, he remained, with his famous Chief of Staff, General von Seecht, in Kurzeme (Courland). With or without the consent of the Allies—preferably with —he intended to attack the Bolsheviks, to advance towards the east, and link up with the White Russian army of General Judenich, and perhaps regain for Germany in the east what she had lost in the west. According to Professor Schwabe his ultimate plan, when he had established his position in the east, was to march with his army on Berlin and restore the monarchy. General von der Goltz's book *Meine Sendung in Finnland und im Baltikum* tells of his ambitions and also of his disillusions. The latter were bitter but he resisted to the end, and had the right to call himself, as in fact he did, 'the last of the German Generals'.

The foreign relations of the Latvians were aggravated by

FIGHTING IN KURZEME

their deep-seated hatred of the Baltic nobles, which has been mentioned. The Latvians desired not only to obtain political independence, but they also demanded a proper share in the national and local governments and the suppression of the privileges of the nobles. Above all, they clamoured for the break-up of the big estates, so that the land could be divided up more equitably. The German Balts, or 'Baltic Barons', were a remarkable race of men, highly cultivated, energetic and ruthless. They administered skilfully the affairs of the provinces and developed efficiently their large landed estates. Their forestry was the best in Europe, and their timber was bid for eagerly in the Baltic Exchange in the City. By reason of their superior abilities they attained to dominant positions, not only in the Baltic Provinces but also in the Czarist Government. A Russian historian writing of the nineteenth century says 'the Baltic nobility turned into a trusted pillar of the Czar's throne, and supplied the cadres for the Court and the highest officials of the Czars until 1917'. The Latvians always associated them with their country of origin, and because they hated the nobles, they hated also the Germans.

Although the Baltic nobles formed only a small minority, 3·4 per cent of the whole population, they owned about 60 per cent of the land; 1,300 of their manors contained more than 5,000 acres each, while the average size of a Latvian holding was 115 acres. Professor Schwabe mentions the manor of Dundaga as containing 175,000 acres, Pope 127,500 and others the extent of which was quite out of proportion to the size of the country. The family of the Barons Wolff owned 36 manors in all, with an acreage of 724,000.

As the Latvians proved themselves to be good farmers, and as they became more prosperous, they wanted more land to own and to till, but, on account of the size of the estates of the Barons, no land was available for them, and there was an acute land hunger among the Latvian agricultural workers. So the demand to possess land became a strong incentive to action in the social revolution. In fact, in no revolution was 'land hunger' such a strong incentive as in the Latvian.

When the structure of the Russian Empire collapsed and the Latvians declared their independence, the Baltic nobles were in a quandary. Their ambition was to maintain their privileged position, but they were undecided as to the way to accomplish this. They tried to keep a foot in each camp, hoping that the wheel of fortune would once more, as it had done so often in the past, turn in their favour. An insignificant minority threw in their lot with the Latvians, but the majority supported a separate militia corps (*Baltische Landeswehr*) formed to protect their interests. They were hostile to the Bolsheviks, but were ready to fight both with the 'White Russians' and the Germans.

Soon after my arrival at Liepaja, I received the visit of Prince Anatol Lieven, a prominent Balt landowner, who had served with distinction in the Czarist army. We talked for some time together in the small cabin of the destroyer (H.M.S. *Velox*) where I was working, and he told me that he was willing to co-operate with anyone who was ready to fight against the Bolsheviks, but he wanted to fight if possible in conjunction with the Allies. He was engaged at that time in the task of forming a small army from the Russian prisoners of war who were escaping from the camps in East Prussia, and he asked me to apply to my Government for the loan of two ships, so that he could transfer his men along the coast to the Bolshevik front. No ships were available, so he advanced overland with his small force and engaged the enemy near Riga. Unfortunately as he was crossing the bridge over the Daugava on horseback, a Bolshevik woman soldier who was lurking in ambush shot him and wounded him

FIGHTING IN KURZEME 45

in the thigh. In consequence he had to retire from active operations in the field and he undertook a lecturing tour, to try to bring home to the people in France and Belgium the dangers of Bolshevism. Later he was able to return to his former estate, where the gardener's cottage alone was free for his use. He belonged to the same family as the famous Princess Lieven, wife of the Russian ambassador in London, whose brilliant correspondence with Prince Metternich, Lord Grey, Lord Aberdeen and other statesmen has filled so many volumes.

Major Keenan and I looked out together on this confused scene and tried to assess the strength of the various movements; certain hostile forces were in opposition and the atmosphere was very tense. The wildest rumours were in circulation which it was impossible to check as there were no newspapers to give the correct news. Usually after lunch we went to call on M. Ulmanis, and discussed with him the happenings of the day. He was level-headed and, as he was admirably served by his intelligence service, was well informed and able to forecast the trend of events. His chief interest had been in agriculture and cattle breeding and he had resided for many years in Denmark. Later he became interested in Latvian affairs and Latvian politics and, as he was a good speaker and organizer and had a good presence, he became the leader and spokesman of the independence movement. His position at this time was that of Prime Minister. During the interviews he clearly showed his disappointment at the failure of the Allies to force General von der Goltz to withdraw his troops from Kurzeme (Courland) and return to Germany. This added greatly to his difficulties.

Later he became President of the Republic and in 1940 he was transported by the Bolsheviks to the Caucasus, where, it is supposed, he died.

In February and March, Liepaja was enveloped in snow and ice, but in April the thaw commenced and grass lawns appeared and women gardeners came and tended the public gardens and prepared the flower beds. The road to the beach became passable and I went for walks on the hard sand, so hard that the German artillery exercised there every morning. At low tide we sometimes found pieces of amber, washed up from a ridge of amber in the neighbourhood. In the centre of the town, the channel leading to the inner dock became free of ice and I penetrated beyond it to the old Russian naval harbour. This had been used in winter by the Russian Baltic fleet because the approaches could be kept clear of ice but now it was entirely deserted. The old naval buildings, the barracks, casinos, officers' quarters, etc., were grandiose, as when the Russians built, they built always on a grand scale. Now, however, not a soul was moving; even the caretakers had abandoned their posts.

General von der Goltz still remained in Liepaja with his staff. As long as the Latvians did not antagonize him, he allowed them to manage their own affairs. He refused however to allow the Latvians to mobilize men of military age in the Liepaja district, and disbanded a battalion so formed.

In the early days of March 1919 General von der Goltz commenced his counter attack against the Bolsheviks and in April recaptured Jelgava, which had been occupied by the 'Reds'.

CHAPTER V

MY MISSION IN LITHUANIA

In April 1919 I travelled to Kaunas (Kovno) in order to establish contact with the Lithuanian Government, though only on an unofficial basis. The more immediate object of my mission was to obtain information on the frontiers claimed by the new state, as the Peace Conference assembled in Paris were engaged on the study of the East European frontiers. I took with me Edgar Hansen, a Vice-Consul at Copenhagen, as secretary, and Admiral Cowan kindly lent me a marine to act as bodyguard. As the journey was difficult, the Lithuanian Minister of the Interior came to escort me and we travelled together by train to Klaipeda (Memel) and thence by car to Tilsit and Eydtkunen. The roads in Germany were still in excellent condition but once across the frontier our troubles commenced. The famous highway from Koenigsberg to Vilna was in any case inadequate for its traffic and as four armies with their cavalry and artillery had advanced and retreated along its wide stretches, some parts were in an appalling condition. In places, the pits were so deep that lorries were buried in them and were lost to view. Fortunately the season was fairly dry and in spite of the ruts and cavities, the springs of the car held out. Eventually we drove into Kaunas, a typically Russian city, built at a crossing of the broad River Niemen. Under the Czars it had been a famous fortress. We were now on the great plain of northern Europe and the surrounding country was so flat that we could see for great distances over fertile rolling country, chiefly corn land, with plantations of pine. The famous primaeval forests which we associate with Lithuania are situated in the east, and were still in the Bolshevik zone of occupation. Everywhere the peasants were working in the fields, trying to remedy the ravages of war, and the whole aspect of this small zone between the rival armies was one of peace.

The Lithuanians had migrated from the Caspian regions in some distant period and had settled in the valley of the Niemen. Here they had prospered and had set up an independent kingdom under a national dynasty, with Vilna as their capital. Later their country had been dominated by Poland and, after the partitions of Poland, Lithuania fell to Russia under whose rule a determined effort was made to break up every non-Russian element in the country and to make it a part of Russia. During this occupation the Lithuanians were obliged to live as one of the submerged races of Europe, but in spite of Russian tyranny they remained conscious of their separate nationality and of their history, and clung jealously to their language, even though for a long period the printing of books in the Lithuanian language was prohibited, a prohibition which was only relaxed in 1904. They always looked forward to the time when they would again constitute an independent nation. In 1917 the Czarist regime collapsed and they felt that the moment had arrived in which their national aspirations could be satisfied and as early as February 16, 1918 declared their independence and formed a Government, with Vilna as their capital. The publication of the fourteen points of President Wilson including the self-determination of all nations, encouraged them to persevere with their project. They were a deeply religious race and as such were shocked by the anti-religious orgies of the Bolsheviks, and because of this and because they believed in individual liberty they refused to adopt the Bolshevik teachings.

MY MISSION IN LITHUANIA

Thus early in their career they incurred the hostility of their powerful eastern neighbour. This led to serious consequences as the Bolshevik troops occupied Vilna and drove out the newly formed Lithuanian Government. The latter withdrew to Kaunas, which became their capital for a period of twenty years. The Kaunas district constituted at the time of my visit a neutral zone between the zones occupied by the Russian and German armies respectively. The population of Lithuania, excluding Memel, was 2,203,000, of which about 84 per cent were Lithuanians and 2·5 per cent Russians. The Lithuanians were a cheerful, hard working race of agriculturists, but lacking clear-cut characteristics. They were devoted to the Roman Catholic Church and to their village life and customs. Their cottages were well designed and well constructed and clustered round the village greens where they reared their famous geese. The arts and crafts which they practised were various and well developed.

At that period the chief landowning families were of Russian or Polish origin and had never been assimilated by the Lithuanians. When the Russians had occupied Lithuania the Czar had rewarded the victorious generals with grants of land in the newly annexed territory, and several of their descendants, either through marriage or further service to the Crown, had greatly developed their estates. As the old Polish nobility also owned large estates, the land was in the hands of a small clique of wealthy landlords. The estates of the Radzivil family, for instance, were said to be so extensive that they equalled in area the whole kingdom of Belgium. The Lithuanian agriculturist was therefore unable to become an owner and as he remained a tenant he resented all the more bitterly the intrusion of these families whom he regarded as aliens. The first move of the new Government was to provide land for the small native farmer, and for this purpose they broke up some of the larger estates, especially those of the Russian 'donations'. They were willing to pay compensation to the former owners but their immediate object was to satisfy the intense land hunger of their people and legislation to enable this to be done was rushed through the Assembly.

As the Lithuanians had declared their independence as far back as February 16, 1918, and as the German troops of occupation had not interfered with their internal affairs, they had been able to build up their state services more quickly than the Latvians. They had elected a legislative assembly, which was in session, their tribunals were working, and the government departments were carrying out their duties, though they were hampered by the fact that Kaunas was only a provisional capital and that their aim was to return to Vilna. During my visits I was struck by the predominance of priests both in the National Assembly and the government departments, which was due to the fact that the education of the ordinary people had been so neglected under Russian rule. The priests, who were trained in separate seminaries, were under no such drawback. The President of the new republic, M. Smetona, was installed in a small palace overlooking the river, and it was here that he received me in audience. As I was the first Allied representative to arrive in Kaunas on mission, and as Lithuania relied on the help of the Western Powers to maintain her independence, he gave me a warm welcome and in simple and sincere words expressed his pleasure at my arrival.

I had several interminable conversations with Lithuanian Ministers about the frontiers which they claimed for their new republic, but they put forward their case in such a halting, uncertain way that it did not carry conviction and so, on this occasion as well as at subsequent conferences, their claims did not receive full justice. In any case, the ethnological divisions between the Lith-

MY MISSION IN LITHUANIA 51

uanians, Poles and Russians were very blurred and boundaries of a geographical nature were lacking.

In some districts the landowners were Polish and the peasants Lithuanian, and in others the population of the villages was of doubtful or mixed origin, one civilization having been superimposed upon another. This lack of clear-cut ethnical boundaries was a source of weakness to the Lithuanians of which the Poles took advantage to claim territory where the Lithuanians predominated. Finally when the Bolsheviks left Vilna and the Lithuanians occupied the city, Polish troops under General Zeligowski in October 1920 drove out the Lithuanians by a *coup de main* and kept possession of the city. This shattered the treasured dream of the Lithuanians to make Vilna the capital of the new republic as it had been of the ancient kingdom. The quarrel embittered relations between Lithuania and Poland even up to the outbreak of the Second World War. It also prevented Lithuania from joining with the other Baltic States and forming a Baltic bloc. On the other hand her relations with Soviet Russia became friendly.

When I reported to the Peace Conference on the subject of frontiers, I suggested that Palaga (Polangen), a small port near the frontier between Lithuania and Kurzeme (Courland), might serve as an outlet to the sea for Lithuanian trade and that Klaipeda might fulfil a similar purpose for Polish trade. The technical difficulties in developing these ports for maritime commerce were undoubtedly great but I do not think that they were insuperable and if Poland could have used Memel as well as Danzig, the awkward arrangement of the corridor might have been avoided. Perhaps even the German attack on Poland might have been postponed. Alas, I never heard whether my proposals were ever seriously considered or not.

Russia granted independence to Lithuania by a treaty

signed at Moscow on July 12, 1920 and Great Britain granted *de jure* recognition at the end of 1922.

I spent my time calling on Lithuanian Ministers, visiting their institutions and getting acquainted with the people. My stay, however, was suddenly cut short, as I received an urgent cable from Admiral Cowan, asking me to return to Liepaja (Libau).

In my hurry to leave, I decided to travel by car, although it was then too late in the day to reach the frontier before dark. Inevitably the car broke down in open country, miles away from any village. There was nothing for us to do but to sit quietly and hope that another car would pass our way and carry word to the next station about our plight. As time went by, we became very uneasy because we were not far away from the Bolshevik lines and knew that their marauders roved about the countryside looking for loot. Our spirits were sinking when, to our joy, a car appeared on the horizon. The driver took me to the nearest village. The mayor had been warned that I was travelling along the road, so, as soon as I appealed to him for help, he sent a rescue party to the scene of the breakdown and next day a wagonette and pair was placed at our disposal, as well as an escort of calvary, and in this manner we arrived at the frontier station. Here we took a train to Memel and so to Liepaja (Libau).

CHAPTER VI

GERMAN *COUP D'ETAT* IN LIEPAJA (LIBAU)

When I arrived in Liepaja, I learnt that General von der Goltz, assisted by Herr Winnig, the German diplomatic representative, had carried out a *coup d'état* and had overthrown the Ulmanis Government. M. Ulmanis himself was a refugee in the house of the British mission. The new Government was composed of Balts, with the German pastor, Niedra, as Prime Minister. The Balts showed great activity at this crisis, and even Balts of seventy were called upon to do military service. The Baltic German militia was greatly strengthened but all in vain as the Latvians displayed their hostility to this government by every possible means. The overwhelming majority supported Ulmanis and demanded his return to power. Without the support of the German soldiers, Niedra could not have remained in office. In his book General von der Goltz explains that he was obliged to overthrow the Ulmanis government because of their opposition to him. It had become clear to him that the Allies were firmly determined to force him to return to Germany. He decided therefore to increase his army, so as to be able to maintain his position in Kurzeme (Courland) until the bitter end. For this purpose he required a friendly government in Liepaja and expected that the Balts would be able to furnish the necessary support. Herr Noske, the German Minister of War, was in Liepaja and disapproved of the new Government because it lacked popular support but he took no steps to alter the arrangements. While the 'fiat' of the German General still held good on land, the British Admiral was supreme at sea and Ulmanis and his companions had only to evade the Balt sentries and take a rowing boat to a ship anchored in the harbour when they were covered by the guns of our destroyers and came under British protection. The Latvian Government therefore established themselves on the S.S. *Saratow* and the Allies continued to regard them as the legitimate government. Each day I took a launch to the ship and discussed with Ulmanis the confused sequence of events.

GENERAL VON DER GOLTZ ENTERS RIGA

It was for political reasons that General von der Goltz had delayed for several weeks his further advance from Jelgava to Riga, but in the first half of May he renewed his attacks on the Bolsheviks, drove them back, and on May 18 entered the capital in triumph. At the same time, he kept a close hold over Liepaja.

Stutzka, the Bolshevik Commissar, had evidently to fly very precipitately from Riga, as when shortly afterwards some member of our mission entered the Ritterhaus they saw his seals and writing paper still on his writing desk. The Bolsheviks had occupied Riga for four months and it was the first time they had governed a foreign city. Their officials had interfered unceasingly with the daily lives of the Latvian inhabitants. Many Latvians were shot and the survivors lived in a constant state of uncertainty, never knowing where they would sleep or eat or work, and this anxiety had rendered them hysterical. They became quite incoherent. The Germans did little to reassure them and restore normal living conditions.

While we were considering the ways and means of bringing the Ulmanis Government back to Liepaja, a complete change occurred in the situation. The conference in Paris had drawn up the terms of peace and had invited

GERMAN COUP D'ÉTAT

the German plenipotentiaries to come to Versailles in May to sign the Treaty. Nobody could tell beforehand whether they would do so or not, but if they refused, it was certain that hostilities would be resumed. Our Naval Intelligence officers knew that von der Goltz had heavy guns in the neighbourhood of Liepaja and Admiral Cowan would not allow his ships to remain in the roadstead as they would be exposed to them, a cruiser, if close in shore, being a large target for a land battery. When the date for signing the Treaty approached, he decided to move his ships out of range and as he was protecting my mission asked me to embark and sail away with the fleet. We cruised about rather aimlessly for some time until we picked up a radio message, announcing the signature of the Peace Treaty. The fleet returned cautiously to Liepaja and the destroyer in which I had embarked came alongside. The quay was deserted and an atmosphere of mystery hung about, but Major Keenan and I disembarked and went back into the town. I called on Dr Walters, who told me to my surprise that General von der Goltz had left Liepaja with his troops and had established his headquarters at Jelgava, a town about 60 miles from the coast. He had feared evidently a bombardment by our fleet and had moved his troops out of range. His departure had created a vacuum and this had been filled at once by a corps of 'White Russians' under the command of Major Kanep. This force formed part of Prince Lieven's troops and had been brought to Liepaja by the Germans to embarrass the Latvians.

The Latvians were in the deepest depth of despair. The hated Germans had left and their old oppressors had returned.

At this moment our military mission intervened, and did so very effectively. General Burt and Major Keenan called on the Russian General and pointed out that the Supreme Russian Commander, General Judenich, was assembling an army on Russian soil at Narva. If the General wished to move his troops to join the Commander-in-Chief, Admiral Cowan would supply the means of transport. The offer was accepted and a day or two later the Russian soldiers clambered on to the decks of three or four destroyers and were conveyed to a Russian port. In due course they took part in the advance on Petrograd.

RETURN TO POWER OF M. ULMANIS

The stage was now set for the return to Liepaja of Mr Ulmanis and his ministers, and even a great theatrical manager could hardly have improved on the arrangements made for their landing. The S.S. *Saratow*, looking quite imposing though rather grimy, steamed slowly into the harbour and the genial Danish pilot brought her to the quay exactly opposite a high wooden stand. The buildings, the squares and open spaces were thickly beset with enthusiastic patriotic Latvians, who cheered until they were hoarse while their ministers came on shore. The harangue of Ulmanis inflamed their national spirit and it was easy to understand by their expressions how joyful they were at the prospect of independence. The three Allied representatives, Colonel Warwick Greene the American, Colonel de Parquet the French, and myself, were invited in turn to address the people. I took the opportunity to announce publicly that Great Britain had provisionally recognized their independence. The government had known this for some time, but owing to the uncertainty about the future of Russia, nothing had been published, and now when M. Ulmanis translated my declaration to the crowd gathered round the platform it was acclaimed jubilantly.

A procession was formed, half military, half civilian, with school children dressed in white and carrying flowers leading the way. Patriotic societies, sporting

RIGA

M. Ulmanis and the Latvian Government land at Liepaja (Libau)

GERMAN COUP D'ÉTAT

clubs, gymnasts with tiger skins on their shoulders, and a great concourse of people followed. Thus Ulmanis and his friends were escorted to the Town Hall. For the first time the Latvians were alone in their temporary capital. The foreign troops had departed.

It seemed to me that Ulmanis would strengthen his position if he made approaches to the Balts, inviting them to nominate one or two ministers for the cabinet, as not only would the Government be more truly representative of all sections of the people, but the Administration would gain if the greater experience of the Balts in finance and business was at their disposal. The feud between the Latvians and the Balts was too deep-seated to allow of any compromise and my efforts at reconciliation failed. Our mission secured for the Balt militia, numbering about 2,000, a short lease of life as a separate corps before it was absorbed in the Latvian army. Colonel Alexander, of the Irish Guards, took over the command temporarily and moved the corps up to the Bolshevik front where it fought with distinction. Colonel Alexander, who was destined to become a famous field-marshal, had arrived with the political mission. His elder brother, the Earl of Caledon, however, was attached to the military mission and in due course was sent to Kaunas. A telegram was despatched in the ordinary way to the War Office stating 'Caledon sent Kaunas'. Through some oversight the telegram was passed on to the Admiralty who interpreted it as meaning that the cruiser H.M.S. *Caledon* was proceeding up the Niemen river to a town some hundreds of miles inland. The telegraph wires fairly buzzed with messages before this mix-up could be explained.

CHAPTER VII

THE GERMANS FLOUT THE ARMISTICE OF NOVEMBER 11, 1918

Meanwhile the fleet of Admiral Sir Walter Cowan, supported by the French ships under Commander Brisson, had established our naval hegemony throughout the Baltic. Indeed it was an historic occasion as never before had the British or French fleet dominated the Baltic. Admiral Cowan blockaded the Soviet fleet in Kronstadt and only once did the Soviet ships make a brief sortie[1]. Merchant shipping could move freely in and out of all the Baltic ports and the main danger was that of the minefields. It was the Allied sea-power which largely determined the fate of Estonia and Latvia.

On land however the situation was humiliating for the Allies. By the terms of Article 12 of the Armistice of November 11, 1918, all German military formations outside Germany were obliged to return to Germany when ordered to do so, but the German Army in the Baltic Provinces refused to return when so ordered by Marshal Foch.

After the Peace Conference had assembled in Paris in January 1919 the Council of Four (President Wilson, Lloyd George, Clemenceau and Orlando) directed the policy of the Allies towards Germany and, when that Council dissolved in June, it was replaced as the 'Supreme Council' by the Council of Heads of Delegations, which acted as the legal successor to the Four. Marshal Foch, as generalissimo of the Allied military forces, received his

[1] See *Baltic Episode* by Capt. Agar.

GERMANS FLOUT THE ARMISTICE

instructions from the Council and dealt with the German Government through the Armistice Commission.

Although General von der Goltz had been placed in command of the German troops in Kurzeme (Courland) as early as February 1, 1919, the Allies tolerated his presence there, as the threat of a Bolshevik invasion of Germany was a real one and it was not until June 18th that Marshal Foch delivered his first ultimatum to the German Government ordering them to evacuate all German troops from the Baltic Provinces. As the German Government failed to comply with these orders, Marshal Foch sent two further ultimatums on August 1st and August 24th. The Marshal also demanded, on three separate occasions, the recall of General von der Goltz but these orders were ignored by the German Government.

The attitude of the German Government at this time was very ambiguous. The German people as a whole were tired of war and were in want of food and all manner of supplies and the Government realized that it would be useless to oppose the Allies and were ready to accept defeat. They could not however impose their will on the military party, who were still strongly entrenched in the War Office and especially in East Prussia. Being unable to restrain the military party, they seem to have decided that they would not antagonize them and they took no steps to comply with the orders of the Allies and continued, even as late as September, to send pay, supplies, arms and ammunition to the German troops in Kurzeme (Courland) and allowed groups of German and Russian volunteers to cross Germany by train to the Baltic frontier station at Tilsit and made no effort to stop them. When, finally, under allied pressure, they ordered the troops to return to Germany, the situation was beyond their control.

The failure of the German Government to order the evacuation of the Baltic Provinces by German troops was harmful to the Allies; their moral influence was diminished by the showing that the decisions of the Peace Conference were not obeyed. Moreover further time was given to the Germans to prepare their offensive.

General von der Goltz had his difficulties. His men considered that, as they had driven back the Bolsheviks, they were entitled to land in Kurzeme (Courland). In fact promises of land had been made to them from time to time by the Baltic landowners and when, at long last, the General ordered his men to return to Germany, they broke into revolt. The mutiny at Jelgava (Mitau) on August 25th was of a serious character and was only quelled with great difficulty.

General von der Goltz had become the figurehead of a wide-spread military movement. In Berlin a Russian-German party had been formed, to give full support to his campaign and many Russians hoped that, with German support, they would be successful in defeating the Bolsheviks. In East Prussia the military party were strengthened by the arrival of active and retired officers from the Western districts of Germany, many of whom had been recently disbanded. The unexpected strength of Poland and the size of the Polish Army fanned the spirit of resistance. General von Esdorff, Commander-in-Chief at Koenigsberg, aided by the Commanding Officer at Tilsit, was one of the chief leaders of this movement. Colonel Bischoff, who commanded the famous Iron Division, was also at the centre of the Baltic adventure. Marshal Foch was therefore dealing not only with a stubborn German general, but also with a military conspiracy. At that time he had no troops available with which to enforce his orders. A proposal to use Polish troops against the Germans was discussed by the Allies but was rejected.

MISSION OF GENERAL GOUGH

The Peace Conference in Paris assigned to Great Britain the task of restoring peace in the Baltic Provinces and

GERMANS FLOUT THE ARMISTICE 61

Finland and General Sir Hubert Gough was appointed head of an important Inter-Allied Mission to carry out their policy. He arrived at Libau on June 18th. Later he established his headquarters in Finland and formed smaller missions to reside in Tallinn (Reval), Riga and Kaunas (Kovno). He also led the Inter-Allied Mission to General Judenich, Commander of the White Russian North West Army. General Judenich also had his headquarters in Finland.

General Gough received his instructions from the Supreme Council and was authorized to communicate direct with General von der Goltz.

When later the two generals met in a small cottage half way between Riga and Jelgava (Mitau), to discuss the withdrawal of all German troops from Latvia and Lithuania, in accordance with the terms of the Armistice, General Gough on arrival held out his hand. General von der Goltz bowed politely but kept his hands behind his back. General Gough in a furious temper and still holding out his hand in front of him, walked straight into the house and sat down at the head of the table. Naturally a conference commenced in such circumstances could not succeed and shortly afterwards the delegates broke up. General Gough blamed Sir Stephen Tallents, whom he had consulted beforehand, for his advice, which had placed him in such an unpleasant position.

General von der Goltz promptly sent an apology and explained that on account of a vow he had taken he could not shake hands with any British officer. For the moment, General Gough was unable to impose his will and had to accept the situation.

The White Russian Army was stationed at Narva on Russian soil, with Estonia in its rear and the Bolshevik Army defending Petrograd in front. Its situation was most unfavourable unless General Judenich could win the support of Finland and Estonia. The 'All Russian Council' which directed Russian policy refused to deviate from their basic principle of 'Russia, one and indivisible' and declined to acknowledge the independence of the border states like Finland and the Baltic republics. In consequence these countries, which had established independent administrations, refused to give any assistance to the 'White Russians' and yet the army of General Judenich, outnumbered by the Reds, could not expect to recapture Petrograd without such support.

General Judenich had several interviews with General Mannerheim, the Commander of the Finnish Army, but the Finns were firm in their decision to reject co-operation with the 'White Russians' unless the latter acknowledged their independence. There can be no doubt that had the 'Whites' yielded on this point and obtained the collaboration of the Finnish Army, they would have captured Petrograd for the 'Reds' would not have been able to resist two armies, one advancing through the Karelian isthmus and the other along the southern shore of the Gulf of Finland. The Allies supported the army of Judenich with arms and ammunition but could not interfere with Russian policy. At this period the General was a tired man and his headquarters were the centre of numerous intrigues, though the General himself was true to the Allies. His second in command was General Rodsianko, who commanded the army in the field, but he was unable to weld together his ill-assorted group of officers and men and form a disciplined army.

SIR STEPHEN TALLENTS' MISSION

An important British mission, headed by Sir Stephen Tallents, arrived at Liepaja (Libau) at this time. Sir Stephen held the rank of British Commissioner to the Baltic States and communicated direct with the Foreign Office. His duties were political and commercial and the

GERMANS FLOUT THE ARMISTICE 63

two missions were instructed to work in harmony, although the military mission reported to Paris and the political mission to London. Both missions sent repeated demands for the eviction of General von der Goltz from Kurzeme (Courland). On this point there was no disagreement.

Much against my will, I was incorporated in this mission, which had been equipped on a lavish scale, and a special ship was chartered to carry the staff and their supplies, including a fleet of motor cars painted with the Union Jack. Scarcely, however, had the advance party started when the Treasury, driven by the nation-wide campaign for economy, took steps to reduce the expenditure and cut down the staff. In any case many members returned to England when fighting broke out in Kurzeme (Courland). Sir Stephen remained in Riga during the German bombardment and the subsequent fighting in the outskirts, and thereby gave moral encouragement to the government. He then served for several months longer in the Baltic before resuming his work in the Civil Service.

Sir Hubert Gough's mission ran into difficulties and the General was recalled.

A French general, General Niessel, was then appointed to supervize the evacuation by the German Army of the Baltic Provinces. This could have been a blow to our prestige but, as long as the Germans withdrew from the Baltic Provinces, the French general made no effort to establish his personal position.

CHAPTER VIII

WHITE RUSSIAN POLICY
TOWARDS THE BALTIC STATES

The policy of Monsieur Sasonov and his 'All Russian Committee' was to restore to Russia all the lands which she had dominated in 1914 and to make no concession to the secessionist states as the Allies, who supported the 'White Russian' forces, continued to do. However, when the question arose in May of granting assistance to Admiral Kolchak, whom they regarded as Commander-in-Chief of all the 'White Russian' armies, the Allies took advantage of the occasion to state the conditions for their continued assistance.

They demanded recognition of the independence of Finland and Poland and of the autonomy of the Baltic States. In other words, they demanded the right of self-determination for the Finns and the Poles, a right which the 'All Russian Committee' had hitherto refused.

In his reply, the Admiral stated that his government felt justified in confirming the independence of Poland but that the Finnish question must be referred to a future Russian constitutional assembly.

As regards the Baltic States, his government were assuring their autonomy. A summary of this correspondence is given in Appendix 1.

Meanwhile, the Bolshevik rulers were prepared to grant full independence to the Baltic States under certain conditions and with certain reserves.

CHAPTER IX

GERMANS ARE DEFEATED AT THE BATTLE OF CESIS BY LATVIANS AND ESTONIANS

Owing to the hostile attitude of the local Latvian population of Livonia, the Bolshevik roving bands were obliged to retire and to evacuate the greater portion of that province, and the Latvians immediately set to work to build up an administration independent of both the Russians and the Germans and to form an army.

The Germans, after the capture of Riga, concentrated their forces in a northeasterly direction and threatened Estonia, while the small Latvian force, under Colonel Ballod, who was still under the command of General von der Goltz, pursued the Bolsheviks and forced them to retreat up the valley of the Daugava. At the same time some units of the Estonian army threatened the Bolsheviks by advancing from Walk in a southwesterly direction, thus helping to liberate a portion of eastern Livonia. The morale of the Bolshevik troops had been lowered by constant raiding and looting, and their resistance collapsed rather unexpectedly. They did not renew their attacks on the Latvians, though they remained themselves in Latgale until January 1920, when the Latvians, helped by the Poles, forced them to evacuate that province.

BATTLE OF CESIS

When the German Iron Division started to move towards the frontiers of Estonia, the German plan became clear, namely to occupy Estonia and establish a pro-German government, like the Niedra government in Latvia. Hostilities against the Bolsheviks were at once arrested and the Estonian army, which incorporated the Latvian North Livland force of Colonel Semitan who had mobilized the Latvians living in Estonia, moved into position to face the Germans. The clash between the Estonians and the Germans occurred in the neighbourhood of Cesis (Wenden) but owing to the intervention of Colonel Warwick Greene and Sir Stephen Tallents, an armistice was arranged. Which side broke the armistice is uncertain, though Sir S. Tallents states that the Landeswehr broke it by attacking the Estonians and hostilities were resumed.

On June 23rd the Latvians and the Estonians threw in all their available resources and attacked the Germans at Cesis (Wenden). The Estonians employed to good use an armoured train and the Latvians were aided by the Cadets of the Latvian Cadet School, who were fanatically anti-German and rushed into the fight, although they had not received proper training. In consequence their losses were heavy. The Germans were surprised by the fury of the attack and retired hurriedly to Riga. Here General von der Goltz endeavoured to man the positions outside the city in an effort to hold the capital but the Allied representatives again intervened in order to prevent fighting in such a crowded area and also to gain time to compose political complications between the Latvians and Estonians. A new armistice was arranged on July 3rd at Strasdenhof, which stipulated that the Germans had to evacuate Riga and withdraw their forces to a line fourteen miles beyond the capital. In consequence the Germans retired on the 14th and the Latvians were then free to administer all the country not occupied by the Germans. Their chief aim was to expand their army, which was again concentrated mainly against the Bolsheviks, though a smaller force was maintained to watch the Germans,

BATTLE OF CESIS

established along a line half way between Jelgava (Mitau) and Riga. Colonel Semitan joined Colonel Ballod and their two armies were united.

General Gough appointed Sir Stephen Tallents to be Governor of Riga pending the arrival of the Latvian Government.

The Latvian Government lost no time in setting out for Riga. The Ministers again embarked on the good ship *Saratow* and sailed early in July for the city which, for the next twenty years—perhaps for the Latvians the happiest years of their existence—was to be their capital. General von der Goltz made no movement and bided his time at Jelgava, barely twenty miles away.

Sir Stephen Tallents considered that it would be difficult for the Latvians to build up the various state services, to organize trade and industry, etc., without the help of a loan, and decided to travel to London to consult financial houses in the City, and to ascertain whether a loan could be raised. Before leaving Latvia he asked me to take charge of the mission.

When the Latvian Government moved from Liepaja to Riga, I also transferred my quarters to Riga and moved into a flat which had previously been rented by the British Consul. Most members of the British mission were quartered in the 'Ritterhaus', a fine stone building which had been the centre of all the interests of the Baltic nobility. They had placed it at our disposal in the vain hope that we could save it from expropriation by the Latvians, but, though we delayed the evil day, the latter took possession of it as soon as we left. It housed the valuable archives of the nobility, and had several large council chambers and two dining halls, one used as a mess by General Gough's mission and the other by that of Sir Stephen Tallents. Old caretakers had been left in charge and they had hidden the beautiful old silver services and china and glass, but brought them out for our use.

Alas, they did not receive the appreciation which was their due, though they were treated with care. I had my offices there.

M. Ulmanis reformed his government and tried to bring in representatives of all parties. The Cabinet Ministers were predominantly Latvian, but three Balts and one Jew accepted office. Their policy was left-Socialist, as demanded by the small farmers and traders, and, except for the large land owners who were expropriated with only small compensation, the majority of the people supported M. Ulmanis, so that when the supreme test came and the nation had to defend itself against the German Army, it fought as a united body.

Riga was a fine and ancient city which had long been the centre for the administration of the three provinces, Livonia, Latgale and Kurzeme. From quite early times German merchants had come there from Bremen and Lubeck to carry on general trade, but especially to purchase timber and flax, and it was a centre for the merchants of the Hanseatic League. The city developed therefore in the North German tradition, with a fine Gothic Cathedral, a number of soaring church spires, an imposing town hall and well built private houses, with steep slanting roofs and gables, the work of highly skilled builders. The whole effect was one of solid prosperity, with a fine appreciation of good and harmonious architecture. In spite of the long period of Russian rule, there was scarcely any trace of Slav or Byzantine influence, and in the general aspect of the buildings the North German tradition prevailed almost untouched. Some of the broad streets and avenues were very fine.

British merchants and British ships had also visited Riga for several centuries and had traded with the local merchants and had carried goods which were sold at the Baltic Exchange in the City of London. A small British colony was settled in Riga and as they prospered greatly

BATTLE OF CESIS

they had built a fine English church, an Exchange, a club, etc., all of which I found in good condition.

The inhabitants were immensely relieved at being free of the Bolsheviks and one felt that the city had taken on a new lease of life. Families returned to their houses and took down their shutters, shops reopened and displayed goods to sell, and restaurants offered surprisingly good meals. Fishermen took their boats into the bay to fish and in the country the peasants worked hard to save the crops. The warm weather of early summer was delightful and several outdoor cafés opened where the people sat and rested themselves, content with results up to date and more than ever determined that they would remain the masters of their destiny.

Rear-Admiral Duff, who was appointed Second in Command to Admiral Cowan, established his headquarters at Liepaja and came often to Riga, and on many occasions his cruiser and two or three destroyers were moored along the excellent quays of the city. There were also several French warships under the command of Commandant Brisson, a loyal colleague of Admiral Cowan. Many of his officers were Bretons, and one of them, Captain Bain de la Cocquerie, became a close friend and often invited me to dine on board his ship. He kept hencoops on a secluded deck and our officers considered this most unseamanlike, but in any case he gave excellent dinners.

The antique and curiosity shops were a great source of pleasure. The Baltic barons were men of discrimination and many had made priceless collections of china and furniture, often English furniture of different periods, Georgian dining-room tables and chairs, Chippendale cabinets, etc. Perhaps owing to hard times the owners had been obliged to sell; perhaps however for reasons of a more devious character, many beautiful pieces had got into the hands of the dealers and, as they were cut off

THE LATVIAN REPUBLIC

from the outside world, they were willing to sell them at very reasonable prices; owing to the difficulty of transport most of these tempting bargains remained in the shops. Amber necklaces were fairly plentiful and fairly cheap and soon after their arrival our officers sent home necklaces to their womenfolk. These proved to be so popular that the officers were pestered to send more, and when their funds ran out one frequently saw them with bundles of old clothes, bargaining with the dealers for amber. Tea, coffee and pepper were very scarce and on one occasion I called on a chatelaine of a country house as large as Chatsworth and, as I was leaving, offered her a small packet of tea. She had not seen tea for four years and was so overcome by my gift that she called in all her maids to look at it.

Commander John A. Gade, whom I had known well in Copenhagen as American Naval Attaché, arrived at this time as U.S. Commissioner to the Baltic, and Colonel Warwick Greene was given other duties. With Commander Gade came Captain K. Castleman and Colonel Holliday as his naval and military assistants. The Latvians accused the American mission of favouring the Balts unduly, but however this may be, the Balts showed them especial favours, hoping no doubt to get favours in return.

General Sir Hubert Gough had his headquarters in Finland, but much of his time was taken up by the affairs of the 'White Russian' army. When he visited the other Baltic ports, Admiral Cowan placed H.M.S. *Galatea*, commanded by Captain Forbes, R.N., at his disposal. He came frequently to Riga, accompanied by Colonel Marsh and Colonel Wilson.

The trials of the Latvians, however, were not yet over. They had still to meet the Germans on the field of battle and to drive them back to the German frontier.

CHAPTER X

GERMANS PREPARE TO MOVE EAST

After the unexpected defeat of the German Army in Livonia, General von der Goltz retired to Jelgava where he schemed and planned to recover his former dominating position. His situation had become very serious and as the difficulties surged in upon him, he seemed to have lost his gift for clear thinking. The German Balts had relied on him and he had relied on them, but they were too few to give him effective support. Moreover, he had underestimated the strength and the unity of the Latvians. An oft quoted remark made by him, 'They are an undeveloped people and from an undeveloped people nothing can be expected,' shows how far he had misjudged them and now he was face to face with a determined nation and a patriotic army, ready to drive his men out of the country. To crown his misfortunes, his own Government were beginning to fail him. In spite of the pressure of the Armistice Commission, they had continued to send him, secretly, money and supplies and they did so even in September, but they warned him that these would cease. It was the prospect of obtaining land for colonization and for farming which had kept the German volunteers together as a compact fighting force. This land had been promised to them by the German Balts, either as a body or as individual land owners but, as the soldiers began to realize that the Latvians would not allow them to remain in the country, they lost their zest for fighting and their discipline relaxed. General von der Goltz mentions that he had cause to complain of frequent acts of insubordination. The mutiny at Jelgava (Mitau) on August 25th was symptomatic of their attitude.

The headquarters of the VI Reserve Corps remained at Jelgava and he maintained his same uncompromising attitude towards the Allies and, as late as September, refused to give General Burt a date for the evacuation of his army or to submit any plans.

He was beginning to realize, however, that his position was becoming untenable and he decided to adopt the plan of placing his army under a Russian commander. He looked around for a Russian General to take over the command and tried to win the co-operation of General Gurko, but neither he nor any prominent Russian would accept the command and he was reduced to appointing a Russian adventurer, Bermondt or Prince Avalov, said to be a Cossack, to the post. On September 21st an agreement was concluded between General von der Goltz and Colonel Bermondt concerning the transfer of the general command in the districts occupied by the German Army to the Commander-in-Chief of the Russian troops.

Although the command nominally passed from the hands of General von der Goltz he still kept effective control and the Army remained overwhelmingly German and drew its supplies, arms, ammunition and funds exclusively from Germany.

By now the Baltic States had become the centre of intrigues and movements and counter movements, largely due to the feeble policy of the Allies. Although the majority of 'White Russians' remained faithful to the Allies, an important group reached the conclusion that, by throwing in their lot with the Germans, they could obtain more decisive help in fighting the Bolsheviks. A group of pro-German Russians was formed in Berlin in close collaboration with reactionary German military circles. It was supported by two former Russian ambassadors, Baron Rosen and Baron von Knorring, and

GERMANS PREPARE TO MOVE EAST

Herr von Berg and one or two German Balts belonged to this group, which met in the salon of Countess Kleinmichel, a well-known Russian hostess. They were active in sending Russian volunteers to Kurzeme (Courland) and recognized Bermondt as commander of the Russo-German forces. Funds were supplied by German industrialists, who hoped to win a leading place in the Russia of the future.

The German military party in Berlin favoured the appointment of General Biscoupsky as commander of the White Russian forces in the Baltic, but Bermondt, who had a considerable following in the army, refused to serve under him and the matter was not pursued.

General Malcolm reported that the Deutsche Schwere Industrie supported the Bermondt-von der Goltz movement and that Krupps assisted Bermondt both financially and with war material. Their object was to destroy Lenin's régime, to convert the Baltic Provinces into a German colony and then to exploit Russian resources for German benefit.

Bermondt's funds were not sufficient for his commitments and one report mentions the despatch of a messenger, Lieut.-Colonel Firstaff, to General Denikin to request a subsidy from his resources.

Money for his so-called West Russian army was printed in Berlin, but the issue of these new paper roubles helped to undermine the confidence of both officers and men.

On August 14th a group of White Russian civilians and officers formed a North-West Russian Government for the provinces of Pskoff, Novgorod and Petrograd which, with the exception of Pskoff, were occupied at that time by the Bolsheviks. The Prime Minister was Lianosow and the Minister of War and Commander-in-Chief General Judenich. The ministers signed a declaration recognizing the independence of Estonia and inviting the Allies to do likewise and established their headquarters at Tallinn

(Reval). Their aim was to induce the Estonian army to take part in their attack on Petrograd.

This government received every encouragement from our military mission under General Gough and from our political mission under Colonel Pirie Gordon; in fact General Marsh, Gough's Chief-of-Staff and Pirie Gordon were the chief instigators of the movement. Their action was *ultra vires* as they failed to consult the British Government and on August 21st Pirie Gordon was severely reprimanded by the Foreign Office though not recalled; General Gough, as military chief, was chosen as the scapegoat and brought home.

The Russian Central Committee in London protested against the action of our representatives and General Judenich complained bitterly about the interference of our officers in the affairs of his army.

M. Shebeko proceeded shortly afterwards to Helsingfors on behalf of M. Sasonov and the Russian Central Committee, in order to assist General Judenich and to investigate the situation created by the formation of the North-West Russian Government. He was unable to bring together and conciliate the various hostile factions which plagued the White Russian communities. They were united in being 'anti-Bolshevik' but otherwise were unable to agree on a common policy and they lacked a leader.

Towards the end of August, the North-West Russian Army, together with Estonian forces, engaged in an offensive against the Bolshevik Army, but they were driven back and the Bolsheviks captured Pskoff.

Another mushroom government to be formed at this time was the Russo-German Government of Count Pahlen, a German Balt at Jelgava. His aim, like that of Col. Bermondt, was to form a corridor between Germany and Russia through the Baltic Provinces and then to attack the Bolsheviks.

On October 8th Col. Bermondt considered that his army

GERMANS PREPARE TO MOVE EAST

was ready to move to the east and, from his headquarters which were also at Jelgava, he sent an insolent message to the Latvian Government, demanding the right of passage for his troops, through Latvia to the Bolshevik front. His plan was to establish his headquarters at Pskoff, which he expected to capture, and then launch an offensive against the Bolsheviks, simultaneously with that of General Judenich.

As the army was under a Russian commander, he seems to have expected that the Allies would not oppose his advance to the east and he caused great embarrassment to the Latvians by his visits to General Burt of our military mission and Sir S. Tallents of our political mission. The latter made the serious mistake of discussing with him his passage through Latvia and the War Office sent instructions that Colonel Bermondt would be allowed to co-operate with General Judenich only on condition that the German elements in his forces were eliminated. Of course his army was predominantly German and his line of supplies stretched back to Koenigsberg and Berlin.

Colonel Bermondt, like General von der Goltz, grossly underestimated the strength and spirit of the Latvian national movement and that was the cause of his downfall.

The Latvian Army, under the active supervision of the Allied Military Missions, had expanded from a tiny force to an army of 36,000 men, but even so was hardly strong enough to hold in check both the Bolsheviks and the Germans on two separate fronts. The Latvians however were ready to expel from their soil, with their own army, all foreign troops were they Bolsheviks, White Russians or Germans.

THE ALLIES DECREE SANCTIONS AGAINST GERMANY

At long last the Supreme Council decided that a more vigorous policy was required if the Germans were to be forced to evacuate the Baltic Provinces and on September 27th they took the decision to apply severe economic sanctions against Germany. They approved the text of yet another note to be sent through the Armistice Commission demanding the complete evacuation of all former Russian territory by all German troops and Germans in Russian formations. At the same time the Germans were informed that severe economic measures were being taken to bring pressure to bear on them until they complied with the Allied demands. These measures included the withholding of supplies of food and materials, but especially an embargo on all German shipping in the Baltic.

The orders of the Allies regarding German shipping in the Baltic were transmitted to the German Naval Commission on October 10th, 1919 and were as follows:

'Owing to the attack on Riga all navigation permits for German ships in the Baltic are temporarily suspended. Ships at present at sea in the Baltic are recalled and no other ships will be given permission to proceed to the Baltic while this suspension lasts. German ships found at sea in the Baltic are subject to seizure by the Allies. Mine-sweepers are recalled.'

Although these economic measures affected the whole of the German nation, they did not cause the military party to alter their plans in the slightest.

Members of the military party continued to send messages to Colonel Bermondt to the effect that he could disregard the Allied ultimatums as they had been sent solely to satisfy public opinion in Great Britain and France, but the German Government had come belatedly to realize that the Allies were determined to carry out the terms of the Armistice and that Germany was in a difficult and dangerous situation. Even before the receipt of the last Allied note, Herr Noske, the German Minister of War, in an effort to find a solution, approached on September

GERMANS PREPARE TO MOVE EAST

26th General Malcolm, our military representative in Berlin and discussed with him the Government's dilemma. He stated to the General that they were determined to comply with the Allied demands but he had to confess, what was already publicly known, that the German forces in the Baltic Provinces were beyond their control. The Government were powerless to secure their withdrawal. He appealed to the Allies for their assistance and assured General Malcolm that the Government would welcome the arrival of an International Commission in the Baltic to investigate conditions on the spot.

The Supreme Council considered the proposal for Allied supervision and agreed to the despatch of an International Commission to supervise the evacuation of the German troops on the express condition that this arrangement did not relieve the German Government of their responsibility under the Armistice. A French General, General Niessel, was appointed head of the Commission, the British member was General Turner and the German member, Admiral Hoffman.

The instructions to General Niessel were:

To obtain information from the German Government as to measures taken for evacuation.

To supervise execution of such measures and to demand further measures if necessary.

General Niessel's Commission arrived in Berlin, where they consulted with Herr Noske, and travelled to Keonigsberg, where their reception was frigid; it was only on November 13th that they reached Tilsit on the frontier of East Prussia and the Baltic Provinces.

CHAPTER XI

BATTLE BEFORE RIGA

BERMONDT'S ARMY ATTACKS THE LATVIANS

Bermondt's army had been constantly re-inforced by German and Russian volunteers, who arrived from Berlin and when he opened the battle before Riga he had under his order 12,000 Russian troops, including German volunteers, and German troops amounting to 40 or 50 thousand men. By October heavy German artillery had arrived at the front and a British Military report mentions siege guns, each drawn by a team of six horses. Two famous fighting divisions, the Iron Division and the German Legion, under the Command of Colonel Bischoff, moved into position on the left flank of his main force. German reserve forces were concentrated in the neighbourhood of Shavli.

It would be difficult to conceive an attitude of greater defiance than that of the German military party to the four successive ultimatums of Marshal Foch.

On October 8th the vanguard of the Russo-German forces attacked the Latvian forces covering the approaches to Riga and drove them back to the suburbs. They occupied a line along the left bank of the river Dangava and the Latvians manned their defences along the right bank. The Germans kept the city under shell-fire but made no attempt to cross the river and the plans of their campaign appeared to be uncertain.

The Latvians maintained their defence posts along the river but lost no time in organizing a spirited counter-offensive. They crossed the river in every available boat

BATTLE BEFORE RIGA

further down at the town of Bolderaa. Here an Allied naval force, consisting of H.M.S. *Dragon*, H.M.S. *Vance* and the French Cruiser *L'Aisne*, stationed in midstream, covered the crossing and fired at the outposts of the Germans in the sand dunes.

The Germans, surprised by the intensity of the bombardment, retreated in confusion. The Latvians pressed forward with great gallantry and attacked the Germans. After a short lull in the fighting, the Latvians again pressed forward with the plan of encircling Riga on the west. They attacked the left flank of the Germans at Regensburg and Thorensberg. The latter was defended by the Iron Division and the German Legion, but on November 10th the Latvians captured the position, together with the enemy artillery.

The German Iron Division was thrown back in disorder on Olai, half way between Riga and Jelgava. This was the decisive moment of the battle, as on November 11th the German troops in front of Riga retreated and their officers failed to rally them and to bring them to stand firm against the Latvians.

The latter again advanced and captured Bansk on November 18th and Jelgava on the 21st, with valuable war material.

On November 15th after his defeat before Riga, Colonel Bermondt placed himself and his troops under the orders of Lieut. Gen. von Eberhardt, who on October 3rd had taken over the command from General von der Goltz. General von Eberhardt arrived at a critical moment as his forces, attacked as they were on their front and threatened by an attack on their west flank, were in a parlous situation. He therefore proposed an armistice, but the Latvians took no notice and continued to pursue the Germans towards Lithuania.

General Niessel was successful in keeping the Shavli-Tauroggen railway clear of Latvian and Lithuanian troops and the railway and the roads were used by the Germans for their withdrawal. He was also able to prevent a German force under General von Nebel from crossing the frontier from Prussia to Lithuania, in order to reinforce General von Eberhardt's army.

At the beginning of the struggle, the Latvians had appealed to the Estonians for their help in opposing the German forces, but the Estonians demanded the frontier district of Walk as the price of their assistance. This district however the Latvians refused to cede and no help from Estonia was forthcoming.

The Lithuanian Government were unwilling to commit their small army against the Germans until it became clear that the Latvian offensive was driving back the enemy. The Lithuanians then cut the railway, both north and south of Shavli and caused great confusion among the German troops who were being driven into Lithuania by the Latvians.

General Niessel's commission intervened at this point and secured the withdrawal of the Lithuanian forces from the railway, so as to enable the retreating Germans to pass through Lithuania to the Prussian frontier. Although the Lithuanians attacked the Germans outside the railway zone they were unable to prevent the devastation of their country, the looting of their farms and the ill-treatment of the inhabitants. The relations between the commanders of the Latvian and Lithuanian armies were very harmonious and there was close co-operation between them.

Although Marshal Foch bestowed great praise on the French General Niessel and his Commission for their efforts to bring about the evacuation of the Baltic Provinces by the Russo-German troops, the Commission, which had arrived so tardily at the Russian frontier, did very little to influence the course of events. It was the Lettish and Lithuanian armies which freed their territories

BATTLE BEFORE RIGA 81

of the invaders, rather than the ultimatums of the Marshal. The Germans were masterly in their bluffing tactics, but in the field they fought badly and without spirit. The chief service which the Commission rendered to the Baltic armies was their refusal to allow German troops from Prussia to cross into Lithuania to strengthen the retreating German Army. Also they kept open the Shavli-Tauroggen railway which was used by the retreating troops. On the other hand they gave great offence to the Latvians by sending a telegram to the Latvian commander, requesting him to halt his troops, which were driving the enemy forces out of his country. Much against his will, Colonel Ballod held back his troops for 24 hours. Admiral Cowan's angry telegram to the Admiralty protesting against the proposal ended with the words: 'I regard this as madness'.

The Germans took with them all that they could seize, horses, cattle, carts, farm implements, etc., and as the International Commission failed to control the frontier, they could not prevent this and the loot was carried into Prussia. General Turner's reports on this subject were very bitter. Prussia teemed with livestock of all kinds, but the rich agricultural province of Kurzeme (Courland) had become a desert.

Before leaving Jelgava (Mitau) the Germans set fire to the historic castle, the castle where Louis XVIII had passed several years of his exile from France. It housed a unique collection of tapestries, pictures and works of art. In order to ensure the destruction of this famous building they put out of action all the appliances of the Jelgava (Mitau) fire brigade. The College Library of Mitau Castle was also burnt and an irreplaceable collection of rare volumes was lost.

Thus ended temporarily a long sustained effort of the Germans to expand towards the east. The *Drang nach Osten* was halted for the time being. In the next period

F

we find that it is the Slav countries which expand towards the west.

DISSOLUTION OF EBERHARDT'S FORCES

The Germans disarmed the retreating Russian troops as they crossed the frontier into Prussia. In December the 'Count Keller' and 'Virgolich' Corps which had fought in Bermondt's army were disarmed and, together with 5,000 other Russian troops, were sent to a rest camp at Neisse. Colonel Bermondt himself was sent to Neisse and thereafter disappears from history.

After their defeat at Olai the Iron Division recovered their fighting spirit and were divided into three formations. They refused to withdraw by the railway and against superior orders marched to Memel, where they remained until January 8, 1920 when they returned to Germany.

By December 8th 1,600 officers, 14,000 men, 1,000 wounded and 390 civilians had been evacuated to Germany, together with guns and stolen property of all kinds, including 3,400 horses.

By December 16th the evacuation was complete.

Smarting under the insults which the commission had received at the hands of the retreating Germans, General Turner complained of the lack of support from the Supreme Council and added 'Their anaemic attitude caused it to become an object of derision. The evacuation has been completed but to say that the mission had been a success would deceive no-one.'

The Latvians claimed damages from the German Government for all the devastation wrought by their troops in Kurzeme (Courland), but only small amounts were paid to them.

DEFEAT OF 'WHITE RUSSIAN' ARMY

General Sir R. Haking was appointed on special mission to the army of General Judenich which began its advance

BATTLE BEFORE RIGA 83

on Petrograd on October 10, 1919. It consisted of about 20,000 men, including a detachment of German Balts, and was supplied liberally with British arms and ammunition and even tanks. The attack was timed to coincide with the advance of General Denikin on Moscow. General Rodsianko commanded the vanguard and after ten days fighting reached the outskirts of Petrograd, but his force was overwhelmed by the superior numbers of Bolshevik troops, rushed to the defence by Trotski. Moreover, General Judenich was slow in sending forward reinforcements. The army was thrown back to the frontier of Estonia, where it dissolved as a fighting force. Great numbers of the soldiers were lost through typhus. How different might have been the result if the Central Russian Committee had taken a more realistic view of the situation and had recognized the independence of Finland and Estonia and had obtained their support.

On the proposal of Marshal Foch, the Supreme Council congratulated General Niessel on the success of his mission. A further proposal of the Marshal that General Niessel should proceed to Reval to settle the quarrel between the Estonians and the remnants of the defeated army of General Judenich was not accepted and the Estonians proceeded to disarm the White Russians who had taken refuge in their territory.

On looking back on this scene of intrigue and fighting, one cannot but regret that our Foreign Office did not take a more active part in directing Allied policy in the Baltic. It was at that time in the hands of two able administrators, both of them ex-Viceroys of India, Lord Curzon and Lord Hardinge, but they regarded the Supreme Council as responsible for Allied policy and time and again they left important questions to the Council where they remained unanswered.

A memorandum on Russia was minuted by Lord Hardinge as follows:

'This is a question which ought to be taken up by the Peace Conference without delay, instead of wasting their time on details as they seem to me to be doing.'

Lord Curzon's minute was: 'If anyone is sanguine enough to believe that this moribund conference is capable in its death throes of producing a Russian policy, I am not that man.'

I should mention, however, that Mr A. J. Balfour, who was a member of the Supreme Council, had written the following minute on a Foreign Office despatch:

'To attribute the apparent and real fluctuations in Allied policy in Russia merely to Allied stupidity and indecision, is to misunderstand the situation.'

When the Latvian troops entered Jelgava (Mitau), they were able to seize Bermondt's secret correspondence which had been left behind in his desk. The papers were carefully examined and extracts were published. These have now been printed in *Documents on British Foreign Policy*. They bring out clearly the desire of Bermondt to collaborate closely with General Judenich but the latter, who was drawing his supplies from the Allies, was evidently unwilling to forfeit this assistance through an association with an army equipped and supported by the German Government.

General von der Goltz returned to Berlin where he was ill received. He was blamed for the loss of so many good soldiers, and also for the economic difficulties which, through his stubborness, were plaguing Germany.

In February 1919, as previously stated, he was appointed to command the German troops in Courland, which were defending Germany against a Bolshevik invasion. When however, in June, Marshal Foch, the supreme military arbiter of Europe, ordered the German Government to withdraw their troops from the Baltic

BATTLE BEFORE RIGA

Provinces, he should have realized that his task was finished, but he refused to withdraw, and by his obstinacy brought disaster on his army and ruined what was otherwise a fine military reputation. He remained too long in Kurzeme (Courland).

CHAPTER XII

INDEPENDENCE OF THE THREE BALTIC COUNTRIES

Of the allied countries which helped the Baltic States to liberate their territory from enemy forces, Great Britain played the leading part. With the presence of our cruiser squadrons in the Baltic, with our distinguished military and commercial missions, with financial loans and the supply of large quantities of military equipment, we gave active and practical assistance in the moment when their fate hung in the balance and during the decisive battle when Bermondt's army prepared to cross the Daugava to attack Riga, it was our ships, together with the French, which opened up fire on the enemy and covered the Latvians when they crossed the river to the counter attack.

We did not, however, take the lead in recognizing their independence formally but waited for them to come to terms with their powerful Russian neighbour. The Treaty of Versailles of June 28, 1919, which dealt exclusively with former German territory, scarcely mentioned the Baltic States and the settlement in eastern Europe was held over for a later date.

Rather unexpectedly the Bolsheviks changed their policy towards the Baltic States and already in the autumn of 1919 expressed their readiness to conclude an armistice with Estonia. Doubtless the resistance of the Baltic armies had been stronger than expected and, as they abstained from taking part in the Russian civil war, Lenin decided that the Soviet troops would be better employed elsewhere. Also he no longer feared aggression on the part of the Germans and did not require to keep hold of strategic positions in the Baltic, for the defence of Russia. He still expected that the Baltic States, without any coercion on his part, would join the Soviet Union.

The Soviet Government's proposals for an armistice were duly reported to the Foreign Office and on September 16th the Latvian Government were requested to take no steps towards peace with the Soviet Union and to conduct their policy as part of a concerted Allied plan. However, our policy was changed shortly afterwards and on September 25th the Baltic States were informed that they were free to make peace with the Bolsheviks if they so desired. Our change of policy was largely due to the heavy burden of supporting anti-Bolshevik forces.

On December 31, 1919, an armistice was concluded between the Soviet Union and Estonia, but the Latvians delayed signing an armistice until the Soviet troops evacuated Latgale.

In 1920 Soviet Russia concluded treaties of peace with the three Baltic States and by them renounced voluntarily and for ever all sovereign rights, possessed by Russia, over the Baltic peoples and their territories. The Treaty between Soviet Russia and Latvia was signed at Moscow on August 11th and granted full independence to the Latvians.

On January 26, 1921 Great Britain granted full *de jure* recognition to Latvia and the other Allied governments followed a similar policy at different dates. The United States Government was the last of the Great Powers to do so, although they had been the protagonists of the principle of 'self determination' at Versailles. Presumably they were unwilling to make a decision until the end of the Russian Civil War. The Baltic States then entered upon their short career as independent nations. In 1921 they were admitted to the League of Nations.

Of all the results of the great upheaval of the 1914-1918

period, one of the brightest was the resurgence, under our immediate guidance, of these three small nations. The Estonians, Latvians and Lithuanians developed small hard-working communities, engaged chiefly in agriculture, trade, shipping and fishing. The people had equal rights with no distinctions of rank or birth and the wealth of the country was distributed fairly evenly among all the citizens. The big estates were broken up and the land divided among the farming community. A maximum of 125 acres was left to each manor. Most of the forest land was nationalized and worked by the State. The general policy was socialistic. The bulk of the population belonged to the Lutheran Church, except in Latgale, where, owing to Polish influence, the Catholics predominated. Although only a small minority professed Communistic opinions, the relations between Russia and the Baltic States were normal and even friendly. The latter in no way obstructed Russian economic life; in fact, the transit trade between Russia and the western world, which passed through the Baltic ports of Pallinn (Reval), Riga and Liepaja, though comparatively small, increased year by year and special facilities were afforded to the Russians to encourage this trade. Wide-gauge railway lines were laid down from the Russian frontier to the ports but the Soviet government took little advantage of the facilities afforded them. There was no ground for believing that the Bolsheviks regretted their decision to confer independence on these countries. However, at some date which is still unknown, the rulers at Moscow decided to reverse their policy and reabsorb the Baltic nations. Fear of the revival of German imperialism under the Nazi Government was the main reason for this change of policy, but also, with the growing economic and political strength of the régime in Russia, there emerged again the traditional Russian desire to expand towards the West. This led the Kremlin to embark on a policy of conquest, a policy supported by those party members who were engaged in spreading Communist doctrines in foreign countries. The Soviet Government then took the decision to bring the Baltic countries entirely under Russian rule and to obliterate completely their national characteristics.

CHAPTER XIII

THE DISAPPEARANCE OF THE THREE BALTIC STATES

The Peace settlement of 1919 was favourable to the smaller European nationalities and it was hoped that they would develop as small independent nations and that this would remove some of the causes for war. The underlying principles of the Peace Treaties were excellent but the authority which was designed to safeguard and maintain the new settlement was insufficient for its purpose. The League of Nations was created as a power to dominate the whole world but when the United States withdrew their support it was deprived of world-wide authority, and even in Europe it became ineffective and was too weak to impose its discipline among the quarrelling nations, to maintain peace and to prevent the outbreak of the Second World War. As it was a German Chancellor, Bismarck, who destroyed the pattern of Europe so laboriously arranged in 1815, so it was another German Chancellor who swept away the European frontiers so carefully laid down in 1918. On each occasion Germany demanded wider frontiers and more power and when, in the summer of 1939, the tension increased between Germany on the one hand and Great Britain and France on the other, on account of Poland, the former made overtures to Soviet Russia and both countries came to an understanding. For some years past the Soviet Government, after having firmly established their authority within the confines of Russia, had been awaiting an opportunity to expand their frontier in a westerly direction and to reabsorb the three Baltic States, a measure which the General Staff regarded as necessary for the military and naval defence of Leningrad. For a short period the interests of Soviet Russia and Germany were identical, as Germany required Russian neutrality while she engaged in hostilities with Poland and the western Allies. She was willing therefore to make great concessions to Russia in order to obtain her neutrality. Both countries agreed to delimit their respective zones of interest in eastern Europe. The Molotov-Ribbentrop Treaty of non-aggression was signed in Moscow in August 1939 and by a secret protocol Soviet Russia obtained from Germany a free hand to deal with the Baltic States. In the words of Lord Halifax, our Secretary of State for Foreign Affairs, 'Hitler, by this Pact, bartered away what was not his property, namely the liberties of the Baltic peoples, a concession which England and France had refused to make'.

At this stage the Nazi Government disclaimed all interest in the Baltic countries and encouraged all German settlers, both Latvian citizens of German origin and German citizens, to leave and return to Germany. Some 58,000 left Latvia and the numbers of those who left Estonia and Lithuania were similarly high.

Two mixed Soviet-German commissions were set up in Riga and Kaunas to deal with the resettlement of these Germans and with the claims for indemnification for their property left in the Baltic States.

Long discussions followed both at Riga and at Kaunas and later at Moscow as to the amount of the indemnification and in November 1940 Count Schulenberg, German Ambassador in Moscow, informed the Soviet Government that the German claims for German property amounted to 215 million reichsmarks in Latvia and Estonia and 100 million in Lithuania. Later M. Molotov made an offer of 200 million marks for German claims in all three countries and counterclaimed for 50 million, leaving a balance in

92   THE LATVIAN REPUBLIC

Germany's favour of 150 million. The Germans accepted this offer as the amount was higher than they had expected. However before the amount had been fully liquidated, the countries were at war with each other.

Soviet Russia lost no time in putting her plan into execution and immediately after the fall of Poland and its partition by Germany and Russia, representatives of the Baltic nations were summoned to Moscow, to receive the orders of the Soviet Government.

Under the threat of invasion Estonia was forced in September 1939 to sign the Estonian-Soviet Pact by which Estonia yielded to the Soviets important military bases in Estonia and admitted a Russian garrison of 25,000 men.

The Latvian-Soviet Pact, also concluded under the threat of invasion, was signed in October. By its terms Liepaja and military bases and certain airfields were yielded to the Soviets. The Russian garrison was to number 30,000 men. Latvia could no longer remain under any illusion as to her fate and at a meeting of the Cabinet on May 17, 1940 arrangements were made in case Latvia should be over-run. Full powers were invested in a representative abroad who would not lose freedom of movement and action in the case of foreign occupation of the country. The representative chosen was the Latvian minister in London, M. Charles Zarine, and as his substitute, the Latvian minister in Washington, M. A. Bilmanis, was nominated.

While the Soviet Government were occupying points of strategic importance along the southern shore of the Gulf of Finland, they were also demanding from Finland military bases on the northern shore of the Gulf, so as to close entirely the approaches to Kronstadt against an enemy. The Finns, whose geographic position was quite different from that of the Baltic nations, resisted the demands of the Soviets and, when the Soviet army invaded

BALTIC STATES IN SOVIET UNION 93

the country, put up a very gallant and spirited resistance. The war which followed is known as the 'Winter War' and in the end the Finns, hopelessly outnumbered, were forced to make peace and yield military bases to the Russians.

The latter, freed from this unexpected entanglement, became still more aggressive towards the Baltic nations. In June 1940 Lithuania was occupied by Soviet troops and Latvia was practically isolated. On June 16th the Soviet Government addressed an ultimatum to Latvia which the latter, owing to the presence of the Russian garrison, was unable to reject. No defence was possible. The Latvians had to accept the Soviet demands, namely the formation of a government favourable to the Soviets, and to consent to the entry of unlimited Soviet forces.

The Soviet troops advanced in two columns, one from Dunaburg, along the Valley of the Daugava and the other from Lithuania, and occupied Riga. M. Vishinsky, the famous foreign commissar, then made his entry on the scene, and, on the following day, called on the Latvian President, M. Ulmanis. Without wasting any time on civilities or formalities he handed the President a sheet of paper which contained the names of the new Cabinet Ministers, as drawn up by the Soviet Embassy, and took his leave. The new Prime Minister was an obscure university professor Kirchenstein, a member of the local Communist party. The other Ministers were all obscure people, mere puppets in the hands of M. Vishinsky and the Soviet Embassy. On July 5th, a decree was published ordering new elections.

In Estonia, where Zhdanov was appointed Soviet Commissar, the Soviet procedure followed on the same lines, likewise in Lithuania where Dekanozov was appointed Commissar.

In each country a 'Working Peoples' Union' was formed which drew up a list of candidates for the forthcoming election. Their list was the only list admitted and the number of candidates equalled exactly the number of seats to be filled. Other parties, with more courage than discretion, put forward their lists, but not only were such lists banned but their authors were imprisoned and probably deported.

The result of the election was a foregone conclusion. All the candidates of the Communist bloc were elected and the sorry farce continued. The new Parliament met and its members unanimously proclaimed the Latvian Soviet Socialist Republic and applied for incorporation in the Union of the Soviet Socialist Republics. On August 5th the USSR were graciously pleased to grant the application. The Baltic States were then formally incorporated in the great Russian Union. Thus these three peaceably-minded democratic nations again disappeared temporarily from the map of Europe to the intense regret of all true lovers of liberty and progress.

Thus the doctrine of the 'Free determination of all nations', which had been advanced with such confidence by President Wilson in 1919 at Versailles and which he hoped would prevent war in the future, was added to the long list of diplomatic failures.

APPENDIX

Note, dated May 26, 1919, from Allied and Associated Powers to Admiral Kolchak, Commander-in-Chief of the 'White Russian' Forces.

The Allies state their conditions for granting assistance to his armies.

Fourth Condition

That the independence of Finland and Poland be recognized.

Fifth

That if a solution of the relations between Estonia, Latvia and Lithuania is not speedily reached by agreement, the settlement will be made in consultation with the League of Nations and that, until such a settlement is made, the Government of Russia agrees to recognize these territories as autonomous and to confirm the relations which may exist between their de facto Governments and the Allied and Associated Governments.

Reply from Admiral Kolchak, May 26, 1919 to the Allied and Associated Powers.

3rd Para.

Considering the creation of a unified Polish State to be one of the chief of the normal and just consequences of the World War, the Government thinks itself justified in confirming the independence of Poland proclaimed by the Provisional Russian Government in 1917, all the pledges and decrees of which we have accepted. The final question of delimiting the frontiers between Russia and Poland must, however, in conformity with the principles set forth above, be postponed till the meeting of the Constituent Assembly. We are disposed at once to recognize the de facto Government of Finland but the final solution of the Finnish question must belong to the Constitutional Assembly.

4th Para.

We are fully disposed at once to prepare for the solution of the questions concerning the fate of the national groups in

Estonia, Latvia and Lithuania and we have every reason to believe that a prompt settlement will be made, seeing that the Government is assuring, as from the present time, the autonomy of the various nationalities. It goes without saying that the limits and conditions of these autonomous institutions will be settled separately as regards each of the nationalities concerned. And even in case difficulties should arise in regard to the solution of these various questions, the Government is ready to have recourse to the collaboration and good offices of the League of Nations, with a view to arriving at a satisfactory settlement.

> Note from Allied Powers to Admiral Kolchak, June 1919.

The Allied Powers welcome the tone of Admiral Kolchak's reply which seems to them to be in substantial agreement with the propositions which they had made and to contain satisfactory assurances for the freedom, self-government and peace of the Russian people and their neighbours. They are therefore willing to extend to Admiral Kolchak and his associates the support set forth in their original letter.

BIBLIOGRAPHY

Latvian Authors

Bilmanis, A., *The Baltic States.*
The League of European Freedom, *Story of Latvia.*
Schwabe, Prof. Arved, *Histoire du peuple Letton*, Stockholm, 1953.
Spekke, Prof. Arnolds, *La Lettonia et le probleme baltique*, Paris 1952.
Walters, Dr. M., *Lettland* (in German), Rome 1923.

Official Documents

Documents on British Foreign Policy 1919-1939
Edited by Sir E. L. Woodward, Prof. of Modern History, and Rohan Butler, M.A. Fellow of All Souls College, Oxford. First Series. Volume III 1919, London, H.M.S.O., 1949.
This volume contains many of the official despatches of the author, written at the time of his mission.

English Authors

The British Society for International Understanding	*The British Survey*, August 1949.
Grant & Temperley,	*Europe in the Nineteenth & Twentieth Centuries*, London, Longmans, 1948.
Newman, Bernard,	*Baltic Background*, London, Robert Hale, 1948.
Pick, F. W.,	*The Baltic Nations*, London, Boreas, 1945.
Royal Institute of International Affairs	*The Baltic States*, London, 1938.
Swettenham, John Alexander,	*The Tragedy of the Baltic States*, London, Hollis & Carter, 1952.

THE LATVIAN REPUBLIC

German Authors

Feldzug in Baltikum. Kaempfe in Baltikum. (Vols. II and III, Jan.–May, 1919; nach der zweiten Einnahme von Riga.) Reichskriegs Ministerium. Berlin, E. S. Mettler & Sohn, 1937, 1938. (A detailed account of the fighting in the Baltic States in 1919 from the German military point of view.)

Avaloff, Bermondt Prince,	*Im Kampf gegen den Bolschevismus*, Hamburg, 1925.
Blücher, Wipert von,	*Deutchlands weg nach Rapallo*, Wiesbaden, 1951.
Goltz, R. von der,	*Meine Sendung in Finnland und in Baltikum*, Leipzig, 1920.
Salomon, Ernst von,	*The Outlaws*, English translation, London, 1931.
Winnig, August,	*Deutsche Ostpolitik*, Berlin.
Winnig, August,	*Heimkehr*, Hamburg, 1935.

Contemporary Memoirs

Agar, Capt. A.,	*Baltic Episode*, Hodder & Stoughton 1963.
du Parquet, Colonel,	*Adventure Allemande en Lettonie*, Paris.
Gade, John A.,	*All my born days*, New York, 1946.
Gough, General Sir Hugh	*Soldiering on*, Arthur Barker, 1954.
Mannerheim, Field-Marshal,	*Memoirs*, Cassell, 1953.
Niessel, A.,	*Evacuation des pays Baltiques par les Allemands*, Paris, 1935.
Tallents, Sir Stephen,	*Man and Boy*, Faber, 1953.

All these authors took part in the events narrated in this book.

CHRONOLOGICAL TABLE

Feb.		1918. Lithuania and Estonia declare their independence.
March	3,	1918. Treaty of Brest-Litovsk. Latvia ceded to Germany.
Nov.	11,	1918. Armistice between the Allies and Germany.
Nov.	18,	1918. Latvia declares her independence.
Feb.		1919. The First Cruiser Squadron enters the Baltic and the Flagship, H.M.S. *Caledon*, visits Liepaja. Author's mission to Latvia. Bolshevik armed forces overrun Livonia and occupy Riga. Later they cross the river Daugava and advance in a westerly direction as far as the river Venta. German troops under General von der Goltz occupy Kurzeme (Courland) and part of Lithuania.
March		1919. General von der Goltz attacks the Bolsheviks.
April		1919. General von der Goltz occupies Jelgava.
April		1919. German coup d'état in Liepaja.
May	18,	1919. General von der Goltz renews his attacks on the Bolsheviks and enters Riga.
June,		1919. German and Estonian troops attack the Bolsheviks and force them to evacuate Livonia and Estonia.
June	18,	1919. Marshal Foch's first ultimatum to German Government to withdraw German troops from Baltic Provinces.
June	18,	1919. General Sir Hubert Gough arrives at Liepaja (Libau).
June	20,	1919. Mission of Sir Stephen Tallents.
June	23,	1919. Germans threaten to occupy Estonia and are attacked and defeated by Estonian and Lettish forces at the battle of Cesis.
June	26,	1919. British ships leave port of Liepaja and German forces also leave. A 'White Russian' army enters and occupies the town.

THE LATVIAN REPUBLIC

June	28,	1919.	The Treaty of Versailles signed.
June	30,	1919.	Ulmanis returns to power in Liepaja (Libau).
July	12,	1919.	M. Ulmanis and his Ministers arrive at Riga and establish their Government.
Sept.	27,	1919.	Final ultimatum of Marshal Foch. Allies impose economic sanctions on Germany.
Oct.	8,	1919.	The German-Russian army, under the command of the Russian adventurer, Bermondt, moves forward to the river Daugava and bombards Riga. Latvian forces cross the river, counter-attack the Germans and force them to abandon their positions in Jelgava and Liepaja and drive them out of Kurzeme (Courland).
Oct.	10,	1919.	Judenich advances on Petrograd.
Nov.	13,	1919.	International Commission under French General Niessel arrives at Tilsit to supervise evacuation of Baltic Provinces by German troops.
Dec.	16,	1919.	Evacuation completed.
Jan.		1920.	Bolshevik troops leave Latgale and thus evacuate the whole of Latvia.
Aug.		1920.	Soviet Government recognizes the independence of Estonia, Latvia and Lithuania.
Jan.		1921.	Great Britain recognizes independence of Estonia and Latvia.
Dec.		1922.	Great Britain recognizes independence of Lithuania.
Aug.		1939.	Molotov-Ribbentrop Agreement to define spheres of influence of Soviet Russia and Germany in Eastern Europe. Germany disclaims interest in the Baltic States.
Sept.		1939.	Soviet Russia occupies strategic bases in Baltic States.
June		1940.	Soviet Russia occupies all the Baltic States.
Aug.		1940.	The three Baltic States incorporated in Soviet Union.

INDEX

Adolphus, King Gustavus, 29
Albert, Bishop of Bremen, 27, 28
Alexander, Colonel; Later Field Marshal, Lord, 57

Balfour, Rt. Hon. A. J., 84
Ballod, Colonel, 65, 67, 81
Batocki, Herr Von, Former Ober Präsident of East Prussia, 38
Berg, Herr Von, 73
Bermondt or Prince Avelov, 72, 73, 74, 75, 76, 78, 79, 82
Biron dynasty, rulers of Kurzeme (Courland), 31
Bischoff, German Colonel, 60
Biscoupsky, General, 73
Bilmanis, M. A., Latvian Minister, 92
Bosanquet, Vivian, 20, 21, 22
Brisson, French Naval Commander, 58, 69
Burchardt, German Charge D'Affaires at Jelgava (Mitau), 38
Burt, General, 55, 72, 75

Caledon, Earl of, 57
Castleman, Captain K., U.S. Naval Assistant, 70
Cocquerie, Captain Bain De La, 69
Courland, Duke Jacob of, 31
Cowan, Admiral Sir Walter, 18, 19, 22, 52, 58, 81
Curzon Lord, British Foreign Secretary, 15, 39

Dekanozov, Soviet Commissar, 93
Denikin, General, 73, 82
Domville, Admiral Sir Barry, 19
Dortmund, Count Conrad of, 27
Duff, Rear Admiral, 69

Eberhardt, German General, 79, 82
Edlund, Sweidsh Lt. Colonel, 37
Esdorff, General, Commander in Chief Koenigsberg, 60

Firstaff, Lt. Colonel, 73
Foch, Marshal, Generalisimo Allied Forces, 58, 59, 60, 78, 80

Forbes, Captain R. N., later Admiral, Sir Charles, 70

Gade, Commander John, U.S. Commissioner, 70
Goltz, Von Der, Commander of German Army of Occupation, 21, 42, 45, 46, 53, 54, 55, 59, 60, 61, 63, 65, 67, 71, 72, 79
Gordon, Colonel Pirie, 74
Gough, General Sir Hubert, 61, 63, 67, 70, 74
Greene, Colonel Warwick, American Representative, 56, 66, 70

Haking General, Sir, R., 82
Halifax, Lord, 91
Hansen Edgar, Vice Consul at Copenhagen, 47
Hardinge Lord, 83
Hertling Count, German Chancellor, 36
Hindenberg, German High Command, 36
Hoffman, German Admiral, 77
Holiday Colonel, U.S. Military Assistant, 70

Judenich General Supreme "White Russian" Commander, 55, 61, 62, 73, 74, 75, 82, 83.

Kalpaks, Latvian Colonel, 42
Kanep, "White Russian" Major, 55
Keenan, British Major, 23, 45, 55
Kettler Dynasty, Rulers of Kurzeme (Courland), 31
Kirchenstein, Prime Minister over occupied Latvia, 93
Kleinmichel Countess, 73
Knorring Von, Baron, 72
Kolchak, Admiral Commander in Chief of "White Russian" Armies, 64
Kuhlmann, Herr Von, German Foreign Secretary, 36

THE LATVIAN REPUBLIC

Laidoner, Estonian General, 20
Lianosow, North-West Russian Prime Minister, 73
Lieven Prince, 44, 55
Louis XVIII, King, 81
Ludendorff, German High Command, 36

Malcolm General, 73, 77
Mannerheim, Finnish Field Marshal, 62
Marling, Sir Charles, 18
Marsh General, 70, 74
Mechlenburg, Duke Adolf Friedrich, 37
Meierovics, M. Z. A., Latvian Foreign Minister, 37
Molotov, 91
Muller Von, Admiral, Chief of Naval Cabinet of Kaiser Wilhelm, 35, 36

Nebel Von, German General, 80
Niedra, German Pastor and Prime Minister, 53, 66
Niessel, French General, 63, 77, 80, 83
Noske, German Minister of War, 53, 76, 77

Pahlen Count, 74
Parquet Du, French Colonel, 56

Radzivil, Family of Landowners, 49
Ribbentrop, German Foreign Minister, 91
Rodsianko, "White Russian" General, 62, 83
Rosen, Baron, 72

Sasonov, Head of "All Russian Committee", 63, 74
Schulenberg, German Ambassador in Moscow, 91

Schwabe, Latvian Historian, 29, 30, 43, 97
Seecht, General Von, German Chief of Staff, 42
Semitan, Latvian Colonel, 66, 67
Shebeko, Minister of Russian Central Committee, 74
Sinclair, Admiral Sir A., 18,
Stryk, Herr Von, Livonian Land Marshal, 37
Stutzka, Bolshevik Commissar, Latvian Lawyer, 41, 54

Tallents, Sir Stephen, British Commissioner, 62, 63, 66, 67, 75
Trotsky, Soviet Delegate, 36
Tschakste, Latvian President, 37
Turner General, 77, 81, 82

Ulmanis, M. K., Latvian President, former Prime Minister and Leader of "Peasants Union", 22, 37, 45, 53, 54, 56, 57, 68

Vishinsky, M., Soviet Commissar, 93

Walters, M., Latvian Minister of Interior, 37, 55
Wallace, Commander, Harrison, R. N., 18
Watson, Captain Burges, R. N., 22
Wilson, President, 33, 48, 58, 94
Wilson, Colonel, 70
Wilhelm Kaiser, 35, 36, 37
Winning, A., German Diplomatic Representative to Lativa and Estonia. Also Ober Praesident of East Prussia, 37, 38, 53
Wolff, Family of Baltic Barons, 43

Zarine Charles, Latvian Minister in London, 92
Zeligowski, Polish General, 51
Zhdanov, Soviet Commissar, 93

For Product Safety Concerns and Information please contact our EU
representative GPSR@taylorandfrancis.com
Taylor & Francis Verlag GmbH, Kaufingerstraße 24, 80331 München, Germany

www.ingramcontent.com/pod-product-compliance
Lightning Source LLC
Chambersburg PA
CBHW061420300426
44114CB00015B/2004